FAITH THAT MAKES SENSE

THE SECOND EVANGELICAL AWAKENING
FULL SURRENDER
CAN GOD——?

FAITH THAT MAKES SENSE

Be always ready to give a logical reply to everyone who asks you for a reason of the hope you cherish within you.

1 Peter 3:15 (Berkeley Version)

by

J. EDWIN ORR
M.A., Northwestern; D. Phil., Oxford

jp

THE JUDSON PRESS
Valley Forge

Chicago   Los Angeles

THIRD PRINTING 1964

PRINTED IN THE U.S.A.

PUBLISHER'S FOREWORD

THE AUTHOR OF THIS BOOK was born in the North of Ireland of American-British parentage and has since traveled through one hundred and forty of the world's countries and visited about two-thirds of the world's major cities. He earned his Master's degree in geography (Northwestern University) and is a Life Fellow of the American Geographical and Royal Geographical Societies.

Edwin Orr is a recognized historian, for his contribution to learning in that field earned him a Doctor of Philosophy degree at Oxford as well as Life Fellowship in the Royal Historical Society; he is a Life Member of the American Historical Association also.

Edwin Orr has written a score of books—travel, history, biography, and theology—which have had a circulation in a dozen languages of Europe and Asia and Africa exceeding a million copies. He is a Fellow of the Royal Society of Literature.

Besides study in four universities, Edwin Orr pursued theological courses in Anglican, Baptist, Lutheran, Methodist and Presbyterian Graduate Schools, and holds three degrees in theology. He has enjoyed a colorful career in the ministry as an adventuring evangelist, an air force chaplain, a co-founder of the Hollywood Christian Group, a field representative of International Christian Leadership, and a world missioner.

His public ministry in recent years has been warmly

commended in Brazil and New Zealand by the Councils of Churches; in South Africa and Australia by Anglican, Presbyterian, Baptist, Congregational, Disciples, Lutheran, Methodist and Pentecostalist leaders. Of his work in North America, Dr. Billy Graham has written: "I think that God has given him one of the greatest and most unique ministries anywhere in the nation." During 1959, Edwin Orr visited again his native Ireland, and addressed gatherings in St. Patrick's Cathedral in Dublin, Queen's University in Belfast, and in many churches and schools, sponsored there by an official United Committee of Irish Churches representing a thousand local congregations.

His unpublicized ministry has brought him into contact with royalty and presidents, with prime ministers and cabinets, with senators and the members of parliamentary bodies, as well as famous people in the professions and industry.

But his first love is for quadrangle and campus, and among students he never expects to grow up. His greatest pleasure lies in addressing fellow students in language that they understand, trying to introduce them to the vital faith which means so much to himself.

CONTENTS

INTRODUCTION

FAITH IS A GIFT OF GOD, but, from the human point of view, believing is a choice. One chooses to believe. One chooses to believe whatever one desires to believe. There are people in Zion, Illinois, who to this day believe that the world is flat. They smilingly reject the evidence shown in rocket-made photographs of the curvature of the earth, insisting that the Bible refers to the four corners of the earth—which is (of course) as much a figure of speech as a commonly used expression "the seven seas."

A student's choice, until higher education, is based on his training—he may have been brought up in a Christian home, or Sunday School, or in Church, or Synagogue, or Mosque, or Temple. As soon as he enters his university or college, he encounters other people's arguments, and may choose to abandon his personal beliefs unless based on a foundation sounder than sentiment.

It is not my purpose to marshal for anyone the profoundest apologies of Christian philosophers, but rather to recount in simple narrative some adventures in thinking which put my own faith to the test and confirmed it. Most of the encounters involved university students, many serving far afield during World War II.

The Greatest Teacher of all time used a method of analogy to convey Truth. He did not adopt a philosophical or theological or mathematical or scientific jargon in teaching—as we understand the terms. Why is this? The answer is simple. The profoundest truth of all, spiritual truth, can best be taught by analogy.

In his lectures everywhere, following such a pattern wherever it has been possible, the author utilized anecdotal illustrations of the points at issue, taking his stories from real life as he remembers it personally. There are obvious imperfections and difficulties in a presentation of this nature. Many analogies may be extended beyond the arc of contact to a circumference of the ridiculous. The same could be said about the parables of the Master Teacher, no doubt.

The lectures which follow were recorded on tape, and were subjected to a minimum of actual correction and alteration, without an attempt to alter the popular lecture form of address. Most essays upon Christian apologetics are heavy in style. These lectures obviously are not.

This volume, therefore, is an experiment and endeavour to see whether a method of speaking—kindly commended by the faculties and students of universities, colleges and high schools—may prove effective also through publication.

J. Edwin Orr

I

FAITH AND THE FALLACIES

A PILOT CAME TO TALK to me in my tent-office in New Guinea, and said: "Tell me, Chaplain, why is any man compelled to hold a religious faith? Could not everything have happened by chance?"

Chance and the Cosmos

I asked him jokingly what he knew about chance and he told me with a grin that he was an expert. So I took out a coin and tossed it, and asked him if it were heads or tails. He replied "heads."

"Now tell me," I asked, "what is the chance of getting heads?" He suggested "one out of two." When I asked him why that proportion, he replied that each coin possessed only two sides, "heads" and "tails," therefore it had to be one or the other.

"What," said I, "is the chance of getting two heads in succession?"

He replied "one out of four." For three heads in succession, he replied "one out of eight" because it was a multiplied chance.

"That's right," I agreed. "It is the probability of the first occasion, multiplied by the probability of the second, multiplied by that of the third."

"What do you know about dice?" I asked him. He grinned knowingly, so I added, "What is the chance of getting a six when you roll dice?"

"One out of six," he replied. For two sixes in succession he suggested "one out of thirty-six" and for three sixes in succession "one out of two hundred and sixteen," and then for four sixes in succession he estimated quickly "one thousand two hundred and ninety-six."

Then I asked him the chance of getting twelve sixes in succession! He allowed me to supply an answer: "One out of two billion one hundred and seventy-six million seven hundred and eighty-two thousand three hundred and thirty-six."

"What," said I, "do you think the chance may be of getting dice to roll the same way all the time?"

"That's fantastic," he said.

"Exactly," I rejoined. "Yet you talk about chance to explain the origins of our complex universe!"

Conversation lapsed for a moment. His silence gave me my chance to expand the argument.

"Let's take something a bit more complicated: take the human body. When your life began, it began as a single cell, which doubled after its fertilization, then became four cells, then eight, sixteen, thirty-two—until it became thousands of cells, finally becoming millions of cells. But from the beginning these cells seemed to follow some kind of plan, each taking its proper place, each following much the same pattern of organization —till finally you were born. They continued to co-operate in a complex organization.

"To send a telegram from Los Angeles to New York, I go to a telegraph office, take a telegraph form, write out my message, take it to the clerk in attendance, pay a certain amount, and leave the telegram for dispatch. The message may be typed out, given to a telegraphist, sent by cable or radio to New York, where it may be decoded, then delivered. Can you imagine that happening by chance? Can you imagine, for instance, the underground cables being there by chance, or the telegraph poles, or the telephone instruments, or the telegraphists, or the pay clerks?

"Supposing I take a pin and stick it into your leg, a nerve in your leg sends a telegram to your brain, saying 'Murphy, you've been stabbed!' Then your brain sends a message to your vocal cords urging them to utter something appropriate for the occasion. Does that happen by chance?"

I told him of an incident on the campus of the University of Washington. After our lecture, an atomic scientist came up to me and said: "Orr, your illustration about the coin and the dice is very interesting, but it is quite superfluous. In physics, statistically speaking, there is no such thing as chance. When one burns hydrogen in oxygen, the result is pure water. When one burns hydrogen in oxygen a hundred times, one gets water a hundred times. When one burns hydrogen in oxygen a thousand times, the result a thousand times is water. When hydrogen is burned in oxygen a million times, the combustion will form pure water one million times."

"That I know," said the pilot. "I know also that mixing hydrochloric acid and caustic soda, two deadly but different poisons, produces common salt. But isn't there an element of chance in the behavior of radioactive atoms?"

I was prepared for his question, so I replied:

"I said 'statistically speaking there is no such thing as chance in physics.' It is true that no scientist can predict which of the atoms of a bit of uranium will break down, but he can predict their number, which is exact enough.

"It is your privilege to believe that such things

happen by chance, and your privilege to believe that the whole amazing universe originated by chance. But it does not make much sense to me.

"A Christian believes that the complex design of the universe is a result of the planning of a Super-Intelligence. This is most reasonable. If you can show me that it is unreasonable, or that any other explanation is more reasonable, I shall withdraw the argument. Chance is less reasonable. So the choice is yours to believe in God."

My pilot friend was such a gambler that his habit reminded him constantly of the arguments against Chance. This so unsettled him that he began to consider what he had heard so often—the reasonable claims of the Christian faith and the good news of salvation.

The Bankruptcy of Atheism

On Morotai, a pilot came to see me, and said:

"Chaplain, I approve of the good work that you are doing, but I do not believe in it.

"Some of these G.I.'s," he explained carefully, "get scared during an air raid, and they need a bit of religion to help them; but I'm an atheist, and I don't need any religion to help me at all!"

"Could I ask you a couple of questions?"

"Go ahead and shoot!" he agreed cheerfully.

"First—do you happen to know everything?"

"No," said he, "Professor Albert Einstein says that scientists, as a whole, are on the fringe of Knowledge. So I'll be quite modest and admit that I am on the fringe of the fringe!"

"Good," said I, "now the second question is this— Is it conceivable that God could exist outside all that you happen to know?" He hesitated.

"How much do you know, in relation to total knowledge—ten per cent?" I asked, facetiously.

"Ten per cent! Less than one per cent!"

"Well," said I, "let us say just one per cent! Is it possible that God could exist outside your one per cent of knowledge?"

"Yes," he agreed. "Theoretically, yes!"

"You're a most remarkable atheist then. Five minutes ago, you stated that there was no God, and now you say that it is possible there is one. Why don't you make up your mind?"

The Inadequacy of Agnosticism

My friend, the pilot, returned to see me a week later —as I felt sure he would. He served as pilot of a pursuit plane, single seater, so he had plenty of time to think on the way back from missions.

"Chaplain," he said, "I've been thinking a lot, flying back. You know, you're quite right, no one knows enough to describe himself as an atheist. I just used the wrong word. I'm not really an atheist. I'm an agnostic!"

"Congratulations," I said.

"You like that?" said he.

"Yes, that's fine!" I said. "Last week, you said you were an atheist—that God did not exist—but you could not prove this, so you were in a weak position. Now you say that you are an agnostic—you do not know if there is a God or not. You're in a stronger position because you're telling the truth—you just don't know. The word 'agnostic' comes from the Greek word 'agnōstos' and that means 'not knowing.' The word was used by Thomas Huxley to describe one who was not bold enough to deny the existence of God, but who found himself unconvinced by the arguments for God!"

Then I asked him what kind of an agnostic he happened to be.

"Are there different kinds of agnostics?" he queried. And I answered quickly:

"Yes, there are two main kinds! Among Christians, there are Roman Catholic and Protestant. Among agnostics are two main denominations, the ordinary agnostics and the ornery ones."

"What do you mean by that crack?" he asked.

"The ordinary agnostic claims," I answered, " 'I don't know whether there is a God or not!' but the ornery one says 'I don't know, you don't know, nobody knows, and nobody ever will know!' I asked you what kind of an agnostic you may be because, if you say you know that I don't know, I'm going to ask how you know that I don't know!"

"Look here," said the pilot, "I quit right there. I'm a plain, ordinary agnostic. But what do you say about arguments for ordinary agnosticism?"

"There aren't any!" I said, provocatively.

"What!" he retorted. "Professor Julian Huxley is a brilliant scholar, and he's an agnostic."

"Granted," I said. "Professor Julian Huxley is one of the most brilliant experts in his field, in biology. But how could any man be brilliant in agnosticism, which means 'not-knowing-ness'? Long ago in Chicago, I took some hermeneutics work. Do you know what hermeneutics is? No? Does Joe here know what hermeneutics is? No? Neither of you knows? Then which of the two is more brilliant in not knowing? You were good in physics, and Joe in mathematics, so which is more brilliant in not knowing hermeneutics?

"So what?" I went on. "Professor Julian Huxley is a brilliant man in biology, and says he is an agnostic, not knowing whether there is a God or not, so we consider that 'brilliant not-knowing'! Imagine one of your professors telling you after examinations: 'You're obviously clever in things you know least about, but you're really brilliant in things you know nothing about!' When a man says he does not know, he disqualifies himself."

"But tell me, Chaplain," said the pilot, "why is it that such brilliant men accept demonstrated evidence in other fields of knowledge, and yet insist that they cannot know God?"

"They won't accept the only evidence. Suppose everyone in a class of students were blind, and a professor announced that he wanted to talk about vision. The students voted twenty-six to one not to accept eyesight as evidence. They thereby disqualified themselves. Some people say that they refuse to accept any evidence whatsoever unless they can smell it, taste it, feel it, see it, hear it, or take its specific gravity and atomic weight. No kind of spiritual experience is accepted.

"I simply tell them: Let us suppose that there is a Supreme Intelligence. What scientific test would you suggest? Barometer? Geiger counter?

"Those insisting that what is commonly considered scientific evidence must be used in all matters theological and spiritual, fast become ornery agnostics. Instead of humbly admitting their lack of experience of God, they began to deny that anyone else may have such an experience."

Militant Agnosticism

I told my friend, this pilot, of a rather painful experience I had while studying at Northwestern University in Evanston, Illinois.

During the year 1941, I took a guidance class in

Historical Bibliography and Criticism. The professor teaching that course took ill and died, and the professor taking his place called himself a secularist.

The professor was an agnostic, a militant one. Perhaps his belligerency was due to the fact that he had been a reluctant candidate for the ministry, had taken a Bachelor of Divinity degree, and had turned against religion entirely. He seemed to take a particular delight in "picking on" believing Christians in his classes and grilling them with red-hot questions.

When he found that he had a Baptist minister in his class, he tried to have fun at my expense. He had given me a paper to write on the topic, "The influence of Geography upon History," and I had said it was remarkable that the world's three great Revealed Religions had begun in the little land-bridge between Europe, Asia and Africa, the center of the land mass of the world. This I thought a most significant fact in human history.

He was quick to object to the implication.

"So, Orr," he commented. "You believe in God!"

I agreed, but said I had not intruded that fact.

"Well then, I want you to go to the blackboard. I want you to diagram your beliefs. Put a dot on the blackboard! And write your own initial 'O' beside the dot."

As soon as I had obliged him, he asked me for a definition of Science. I fumbled.

"Sir," I said, "Science is—Science is——We both know what Science is!"

"Listen, Orr," said he, "I want to know what you think it is!"

I told him that I considered Science to be the realm of proven fact or demonstrated knowledge. The professor accepted the word "knowledge," and asked if there were limits to such knowledge. When this was agreed, he asked me to take chalk and draw a circle on the blackboard around the dot, theoretically inclosing all of Science, the realm of knowledge. I was then asked to give an example of a scientific fact. So I suggested that oxygen was twenty-one per cent of the atmosphere. (I had demonstrated this in our physics laboratory.)

"Agreed," said the professor. "Now, Orr, inside that circle is every known fact and item of knowledge. Is God inside that circle or outside?"

I suddenly realized that I was on the horns of a dilemma. If I claimed that God was within the circle of scientific knowledge, he would ask me to prove the existence of God the way one proves the existence of oxygen! That cannot be done.

So I wrote the letter "G" outside the circle. The professor was truly delighted. He repeated that God was outside the realm of knowledge—our accepted definition of Science.

He told me with the heaviest of sarcasm that almost anyone could think about God, could talk about God, could preach about God, could pray to God, but how could anyone really know God?

Not being much of a philosopher, I stood and stared at the blackboard and the diagram forced upon me. While the class sniggered, I began to re-examine the premises of the argument, and test the basic ideas. It suddenly struck me that I had been forced to accept wrong premises.

Talking about working on the wrong premises, there was once a fellow busy in California completing his doctoral thesis on alcoholism—what makes some folk get drunk. He found an eager rascal on Skid Row willing to do all necessary field research for him for nothing but the raw materials for the experiment.

The zealous fellow got drunk on Mondays with whisky and soda, on Tuesdays with rum and soda, on Wednesdays with brandy and soda, on Thursdays with gin and soda, and on Fridays (in spite of Senator McCarthy) with vodka and soda!

The researchist asked himself: What is the common denominator? What gets him drunk? It was obviously the soda! Such scientific jargon sounded convincing, but it was sheer nonsense.

People will accept a pseudo-scientific theory—provided it is couched in scientific language—with never a thought of examining the premises.

I looked at my diagram again. What was wrong with it? What right had the professor to make me place myself as a little dot within the realm of science in the first place? It is quite true that following cremation, my ashes could be sold to a chemist for the carbon, calcium and phosphorus in them for very little. Is that all there is of me?

When Winston Churchill stood in London and declared: "We shall fight on the beaches, we shall fight in the streets, we shall never surrender——" what chemical formula said that? That was the spirit of Sir Winston Churchill. And what is the specific gravity of a spirit? Nobody can say.

So I took my chalk and extended the dot into an axis outside the circle—for though my body and things pertaining thereto are known to Science, Science can say nothing about things spiritual.

Therefore I joined the axis, representing myself outside the circle of science, to the symbol representing God, by means of an arrow. It is in my spirit that I know God. I had unwittingly diagrammed the statement of Jesus Christ: ". . . those who worship him must worship in spirit and truth."

It is impossible to know God any other way, because God is a Spirit, and spiritual truth is only spiritually discerned.

Science versus Religion?

"Does anything in geology hinder one believing in God?" I asked my tutor in that department.

"Certainly not," replied my professor. "Geology is a study of the crust of the earth, and one would not find God among the sedimentary rocks!"

I asked a chemist the same sort of question, and he replied that, as chemistry is a study of the elements and their compounds, one would not expect to find God in a test tube. One might add that not one branch of science, from astronomy to zoology, contradicts the idea of God.

At the conclusion of a lecture on campus, a student once said to me:

"Why is it that you religious people can't prove anything? A biologist can take you to his microscope, and an astronomer to his telescope, but you religious people are always speaking about taking things by faith."

"Man," said I, "can't you see that true faith is a kind of eyesight? Just suppose this whole class were blind from birth, and I had been asked by the professor in charge to deliver a lecture on 'Color.' I begin by saying: 'Gentlemen, color is a manifestation of light . . .' Up goes a hand, 'Sir, before we go any further, what is light?' I reply: 'Don't you know what light is!' 'No.' 'Well,' I explain, 'light is a kind of radiation. You know what heat is? Well, just as heat radiates warmth, light makes things visible.' Another hand is raised: 'What is visible?' I explain that visible means 'able to be seen' but this means nothing to anyone in the audience.

"I go on: 'If light from the window strikes a prism of glass, it breaks up into a spectrum of color on the wall, like a rainbow.' Up goes another hand: 'Sir, what is a rainbow?' I explain again: 'A rainbow is caused by the refraction of the sun's rays in a rain cloud! A rainbow is red and blue and green. Red is the color of blood; blue is the color of the sky; green is the color of grass!' But no blind student has ever seen any color. I say that the essential characteristic of red is reddishness. A student inquires: 'Is it possible to describe color in scientific words without referring to the context of eyesight?' I explain that a Swedish scientist named Angstrom measured the wave length of light. Red is seven thousand Angstrom units; blue is four thousand eight hundred Angstrom units. Do you think for a moment that all the 'blind-from-birth' students would nod their heads, in appreciation of this explanation in the exact language of science? Do you not agree that a poor old washer-woman with the blessing of eyesight knows more about color than a blind mathematician? So a washer-woman with the perception of faith in God knows more about the 'why?' of the universe than the most brilliant unbeliever."

The God of Imagination

I reported for duty September 1944 on the island of Morotai, then the farthest-advanced base in the Pacific Theater of Operations. We landed on D-day plus 3, but our first few days were devoted to self-preservation on account of the recurring Japanese air raids.

My tentmate was a medical officer, an obstretrician from Philadelphia. We kept our minds off the air raids at night by discussing in a foxhole the problems of politics, science, philosophy and religion. One midnight, the medical officer said:

"Now listen, Chaplain! God is nothing more than an idea in people's minds. If you were to talk to a Solomon Islander, and ask him about a God, he thinks the thunder is God. But go to India and talk to an Indian peasant—he can explain the thunder, yet when an epidemic breaks out, he blames it on God and rushes to burn incense in his temple. Travel down to Australia and you find an educated Australian who explains both thunder and epidemics, yet uses the term God to cover up what he cannot understand. What I am trying to say is that the farther you push back the frontiers of knowledge, the less you need an idea of God. God exists only in people's minds."

"You mean," said I, "that if the whole human race were destroyed in a catastrophe, God would cease to exist? Well, I would like to take up the analogy you have given. Supposing you talk to a Solomon Islander, and ask him: 'Have you ever heard of King George?' He replies: 'Yes, me British subject, me belong King George!' But you say: 'How do you know that there is such a person as King George? Have you ever seen King George?' The simple islander says: 'No, but me British subject, me belong King George.'

"Then you say: 'Well, what do you think King George is like?' That's a fair question. In the Solomon Islands, the chief of a village has four wives and the chief of an island has forty wives. The islander suggests that King George is a very big chief with four thousand wives, which is a rather primitive idea of constitutional monarchy, don't you think?

"Travel from the Solomon Islands to India and ask an Indian peasant whether he has ever seen King George, and what he is like. He thinks in terms of a local rajah, a neighboring maharajah or of the Mogul Emperors, so he says that King George is the British Raj, the Emperor of India. His concept is of a higher order.

"Down in Australia, they have a clearer idea. An Australian says: 'You Yanks don't understand monarchy. The King doesn't rule us, he reigns. He is the symbol of the Commonwealth. He doesn't tell us what to do. We rule ourselves as much as you do or anyone else. We are a free and democratic people.'

"Then you go to London to meet someone who says that he went to Cambridge University with King George, when he was a young prince. He thinks of the King as an undergraduate.

"At a court function in London, you are glad to meet Princess Elizabeth, who talks of her royal father as 'Daddy.'

"Then you talk next to an American tourist, who tells you cheerfully: 'It's all right for the Limeys to have a king, but we don't need one in America, although we have no objection to their having one.'

"And, finally, you talk to a Russian describing the King as 'catspaw of the capitalist system,' so that Communists must destroy the monarchy in Britain as in Russia, in his opinion.

"Seven different ideas of King George! But an important thing to remember is that, if there is such a person as King George, seven different ideas do not change his character.

"Throughout the world of humanity, there may be a thousand and one ideas of God, but, if there is a God, these ideas do not change His character."

There was a long silence before the all clear sounded. We clambered out of the foxhole.

"Then," said my friend, the doctor, "how is anyone to know anything at all about God?"

"We only know as much as He chooses to disclose. We believe that He has chosen to present Jesus Christ as the living photograph of God."

II

AN ARGUMENT FOR GOD

IS IT POSSIBLE TO PROVE that there is a God? No, it is not possible if by proof one means scientific proof. What scientific tests could anyone use? Litmus paper, spectograph, Geiger counter? No. But it is possible to show that faith in God is most reasonable, and that alternative views are less reasonable. How may we do so?

In intelligent discussion, one must start with a measure of agreement. I remember, when our children were very much younger, hearing an argument between my son and daughter. Said my daughter: "I tell you it is!" And my son retorted: "I tell you it's not!" Said she: "But it is!" and he replied: "But it isn't!" So my daughter observed: "You know nothing!" And my son repeated: "You know nothing!" Said she: "Listen to the copy cat!" He chortled: "Listen to the copy cat!" Said she: "Oh, shut up!" He replied: "You shut up!" I said: "Both of you shut up!"

They were not trying to discover any truth—they were just arguing. And many such arguments occur among grown-up people too. When I was crossing the Pacific Ocean with eight thousand American soldiers bound for Guadalcanal, I was involved one night in an argument with a rude atheist from Brooklyn. I can stand atheists, and I can stand people from

Brooklyn, but atheists from Brooklyn are very hard to take.)

"Go on, Chaplain," said he, "you don't believe all that, do you?"

"Of course I do," I replied. Then I added: "Do you believe in the Bible?"

"The Bible is only a book!" he retorted.

"It's an inspired book," I said.

"That's what you say," he said.

"Well, then," I asked, "you believe in Christ?"

"Christ is dead," he retorted.

"He rose again from the dead," I replied.

"That's what you say," he jeered.

"Well," said I, "do you believe in God?"

"No," he replied, "I'm an atheist!"

"What do you believe, then?"

"I believe," he retorted, "that all religion is a racket!"

"No, it's not," I protested.

"Yes, it is," he insisted.

"That's just what you say!" said I.

And there we were, just like a couple of kids, arguing about nothing. Rather let us suppose we engaged in a debate with an unbeliever in this style and manner:

"Now, sir, we differ on many points, don't we? But we ought, as you agree, to have an exchange of views. Isn't there anything that we agree on?"

Where would we best begin? Surely there is common ground somewhere?

The Axiom of Existence

The very first point of agreement is, I think, the axiom of existence. I believe that I exist, and he believes that he exists. This is an axiom, a truth so self-evident that no amount of reasoning can make it any plainer, though some deny it.

I was speaking at California Polytechnic, when a student rose to say he did not accept "existence" as an axiom, rather an illusion of the five senses.

"It's strange," said I, "that you have come all the way from your home to study in California, and you're not sure whether you're here or not!"

But I knew what he meant. One of our planes crashed at Morotai. It was my sad duty to bury some of the men who were killed as well as help some who were badly burned. One man was dying and I was reading to him from the Twenty-third Psalm, when suddenly he called out:

"Open the window, doc. It's awful stuffy here."

The poor fellow was out in the open air in a temporary casualty ward of the hospital. He had not heard me, because he was deaf. He had not seen me, because he was blind. Presumably, he had lost his senses of taste and smell. The only sense left to him was his sense of touch which he was losing fast, soon lapsing into a coma, and that was the end of this life for him. He was still alive, but life did not mean a thing to him, for he had lost the use of his five senses.

The Fact of Order

Can we go any further? Can a believer and an unbeliever find further common ground? Yes, we believe in the fact of rational order or pattern in the universe. Every scientific achievement of recent years has been planned on the premise of order. It was necessary to study the ordered movement of the moon in order to launch a rocket in that direction. It runs like clockwork, as do the tides. We find this order everywhere we look around us, with microscope or telescope.

There are some people who question this universality of order. At the University of Adelaide, the president of the Rationalist Club asked me:

"Sir, are you not just choosing facts that suit your argument? Is there not a great deal of chaos in the universe? For example, in the air in this room, the molecules are bombarding each other in every possible way in a most chaotic fashion. There is no order there!"

"On the contrary," I replied, "this very chaos in diffusion of gases is an argument for design! If it were not for such diffusion of gases, all the carbon dioxide would collect around me, and I would drop dead while talking to you. If it were not for the diffusion of gases, certain gases poisonous to human life would collect in one place, and life would be an impossibility. This order is a powerful argument for purposeful design."

The Hypothesis of a Designer

An axiom is universally accepted, and a fact may be observed or demonstrated. What hypothesis may we use to explain the fact of order?

Is it necessary to explain the fact of order? I walked along a Queensland beach, quite lost in thought, until I happened upon a puddle of water in the exact shape of Australia. I did not give it much thought, feeling sure that a hollow of sand had been filled by the retreating tide. But ten paces away, I found another map of Australia, and another, and another. I felt compelled to find an explanation for the series. Next day, I found an Aussie lad with bucket and spade responsible!

Moving out to Sansapor in New Guinea, we left behind us a jeep. A Papuan native, who had never seen a jeep before, came down the mountain. Not only had he never seen a jeep; he had never seen a wheelbarrow! His wife following him asked: "What is this?" He replied: "I do not know!" "What is it called?" "I do not know!" "What does it do?" "I do not know!" "Where did it come from?" All he could answer was: "I do not know!"

One thing he recognized was the seat, so he sat on it. He turned the steering wheel; he blew the horn; he pulled on the brakes; he let them off again; he changed gears; he opened the glove compartment; but he understood nothing of it.

He happened to touch the self-starter button. The jeep had been left in gear, so it rocked him. That did not make much sense. He examined a few other devices, then touched the self-starter button again. It rocked him a second time. The third time he tried it, he happened to have his foot heavily on the clutch pedal, so the engine started up front. He had never heard an engine before. It sounded like a great cat purring, so he thought he would get out and run around the front to see what was making the noise. When he did so, the engine stalled. He got back in again. He tried to start it again. It just rocked him. Then he remembered to put his foot heavily on the clutch.

He decided to let his foot off that clutch pedal slowly enough to give him time to run to the front to see what was making the noise. As he did so, the whole jeep moved forward with him. He was driving—very much against his will. He dived out of the vehicle, and did not return for half an hour.

But, when he did return, he discovered that he could drive! His wife hid behind the nearest tree while he drove the jeep right across the clearing, where he stuck against a tree until he stumbled upon the reverse gear. He had learned to drive.

His wife asked again: "What is it?" He replied: "I do not know!" Again: "What is it called?" "I do not know!" "What does it do?" "It goes by itself!" "Where does it come from?" He replied: "I do not know. But whoever made this thing must be a lot more intelligent than I am!"

(Of course, it must be admitted that a savage could be educated to understand the workings of an automobile. He could, even, with the help of others, become skilled enough to build one. Our scientists likewise have become more informed about the workings of the universe, and more ingenious in inventing things within its laws, but they lack the supreme intelligence and mighty power of God.)

We look at the universe, and all we can say is that: Whoever made it must be much more intelligent than we are, than the population of this city, than the population of this country, or the population of this world. In fact, this Supreme Being, Who brought the universe into being must be much more intelligent than all the human race.

Some people call Him the Great Architect. Others call Him the First Great Cause. We call Him God. And this is the most reasonable of the explanations of the design—a designer. Someone may say that to follow an axiom and a fact with an hypothesis is weakening the argument. Quite the contrary! Most scientific discoveries are made on a basis of hypothesis. This hypothesis of a Designer is most reasonable. There is not any explanation more reasonable.

Nevertheless, agreement upon the reasonable hypothesis of a Designer by no means solves the problem for the inquirer. Some who believe the fact of a Designer are vague about His nature.

The Perils of Pantheism

There are some people who believe that God is nothing more than an intelligent and voluntary yet wholly impersonal "substance," identified with the totality of the universe, hence the word "pantheism," meaning "all is God."

"Of course, I believe in God," said an Indian to me. "God is the all in all things. God is light, and God is darkness. God is warmth, and God is cold. God is near, and God is far. God is good, and God is evil. All that exists and everything that happens is God."

"You mean," said I, "that God is the universe. Is the universe eternal—how then do you account for the second law of thermodynamics? And is the universe perfect—how then do you account for the evil we all see? Or if all things are equally expressions of God, all things should be equally admirable. Every day, we see around us actions good and commendable —reflecting God. But when we see actions we can describe only as wicked and deplorable, we cannot blame a perfect God."

My Indian friend protested that he did believe in an infinite God.

"Yes," I objected, "you lock him up in a finite universe. Besides, if I were to judge from the world around us, I would say that your pantheist God is not yet made —he is in the process of being manufactured. You say that we are all parts and particles of God. Yet I know that I, most surely, am not God. My conscience protests against such a presumption. God is over all and in all, that's true; therefore He cannot be the universe.

He is over, and He must be distinct from the universe He moves in, as I am distinct from the shoes I walk in."

Could an impersonal God produce beings self-conscious and free? If the Creator includes in himself all good and evil, why should any creature be held responsible for his actions?

It was not difficult to tell my inquiring Indian friend that I had always held Mahatma Gandhi in greatest respect. How could I believe in a God inferior in morality to Gandhi, as do some, who hold a pantheistic interpretation?

In India, there are people living in strictest honesty. There are also folk who worship God by thieving. There are people of the highest sex-purity. There are also those who worship God by debauchery. When pantheism is let prevail, it soon degenerates into idolatry. People begin to worship the god of the sky and the god of the wind and the god of the sea and the god of health and the god of disease and the god of purity and the god of impurity. The worshiper kneels before a gaudy wooden idol. The idol seems so near, yet the god is so far away. The true God seems so far away, yet He truly is near. Pantheism begets idolatry and degradation.

The Defects of Deism

Some people will grant the existence of God, but deny that He is knowable or approachable.

On one occasion, I had been conducting Divine service on board a landing ship, for the Protestant men first, then for the Roman Catholic men, by a papal dispensation. A Colonel of the United States Army was leaning over the taffrail of the invasion ship, discussing the address given.

34

"I enjoyed your talk, Chaplain," he said, adding, "I believe in the existence of God, but I don't believe in Jesus Christ, or in prayer, or anything like that. I believe that God created the universe. He set the ball rolling, so to speak. But I don't believe God interferes in things. He delegates His authority to nature, in a chain of command."

"You will be interested to know," I said, "that your point of view is the same as that of Thomas Jefferson, who was a deist like yourself."

"Well," said the Colonel, "I'm glad to hear I'm in such good company. Let me explain, Chaplain. General MacArthur is in full command of this theater of war. Now supposing Sergeant Joe Blow wants a furlough to go to San Francisco to see his girl friend. He won't get by his captain, let alone see General MacArthur. General MacArthur is ultimately responsible for Sergeant Joe Blow, but General MacArthur is too big and too busy to be bothered with Joe Blow or his affairs. Now, do you agree? I'm sure you do."

When I nodded, the Colonel went on:

"Well, that's my idea of God. God is ultimately responsible for us all, but He has delegated His authority to Nature, therefore He could not be interested in our petty affairs. He is much 'too big' and 'too busy.'"

"Colonel," I said, "there is a young fellow named Arthur MacArthur, and I'm quite sure he has the right to go see his father any time he desires. And even if his father were busy, he would say: 'Gentlemen, I would like you to meet my son, Arthur.' He is his child. And the great message of Jesus Christ is simply that God is our Father and that we may have access to God through Him."

Deism denies the immanence of God, just as pantheism denies God's transcendence. Deism and pantheism discourage real fellowship with an intelligent and loving Creator.

There are other systems of thought and worship, such as the Shinto doctrine of Henotheism—a tribal or national god—and the practice of polytheism, found among the Greeks and Romans of history and among other peoples in the world of today. Henotheism and polytheism have little appeal to the modern mind, but pantheism may be found in popular pseudo-Christian forms. Its main thesis is that God is expressed in Man, the highest of His creatures. Self-realization is the way to discover God, they say.

The Question of Revelation

If there is a Supreme Being, as a majority of the world's inhabitants believe, could He communicate with me? Could a Supreme Intelligence communicate with a minor one? Why not?

In addressing English-speaking students, one uses the English tongue. To address students unfamiliar with English, an interpreter is needed.

Some people have been more aware than others of God. Some became His spokesmen or prophets. Divine revelation has been written down for us, and translated into a multitude of tongues. The Holy Scriptures are a record of God's dealings with mankind. The Old Testament tells of His preparation of a chosen people; the New Testament records the life and teachings of Christ.

A sergeant asked me what I meant by "the revelation of God in the Scriptures"—"Isn't the Bible only a book?" I told him that, when I visited Soviet Russia, in 1935, a man could get married on the tenth of the month, take his bride to a hotel for a honeymoon, kiss her goodbye on the morning of the thirteenth, go down to the divorce bureau and divorce her. He did not even need to go back to tell the girl, for the office sent her a post card.

Twelve years later a professor from behind the Iron Curtain visited me at Oxford University and said that it had become extremely difficult for anyone to get divorced in Russia. Why? Girls had been committing suicide; babies were being abandoned; social diseases were increasing; and children were turning into juvenile delinquents by the million. The Soviet government wisely put a stop to the abuses, and decreed an end to easy divorce. All governments agree that marriage must be protected to ensure a happy society.

But, thousands of years ago, Moses said: "You shall not commit adultery!" which stresses this sanctity of the marriage relation. A family should be a closed unit. A man should be loyal to the woman that bears his children, and a woman to the man that fathers her children.

In 1935, during that visit to Russia, I noticed that one day in seven was not kept as a holiday. Workers took off the sixth, the twelfth, the eighteenth, the twenty-fourth, and the thirtieth of any month. Why? The French Revolutionists tried one day in ten for the same reason. It was a blow at organized religion. In Russia, godly Moslems could not go to the mosque on Fridays more than eight times a year; godly Jews could not go to synagogue on Saturday more than eight times a year; and godly Christians could not go to church on Sunday more than eight times a year. Now the Russians have returned to one day off in seven.

During the blitz, the Royal Factory Commission in Britain—trying to discover a way of obtaining maximum efficiency of willing workers—found that men who worked six days and took one day off did better work than men working in any other pattern whatsoever. But the Bible taught: "Six days you shall labor, and do all thy work; but the seventh day is a sabbath of the Lord your God; . . ."

We who are Christians believe that God has revealed Himself primarily in the Holy Scripture, supremely in Jesus Christ. The greatest figure of history was no ordinary man. He revealed the character of God in a way utterly unsurpassed—certainly never matched in any other religion.

Confucianism is a code of ethics devised by a great teacher; Buddhism is a philosophy of life propounded by a great thinker; but the religions which claim Revelation are Judaism, regarded by Christians as a preparation for Christ, and Christianity itself as the revelation of God in Jesus Christ, followed by Islam, considered by Christians an aberration from Judeo-Christianity.

The Test of Experience

An axiom! A fact! An hypothesis! A question? The hypothesis may be tested by experience. Who comes to God must first believe that He exists, that He rewards those who diligently seek Him. Those of us who have taken the trouble to put this to the test have found it to be true. It has brought us into fellowship with the Maker of the Cosmos.

III

"OF HEAVEN AND EARTH"

CHRISTENDOM'S MOST CLEAR-CUT CREED describes Almighty God as Maker of heaven and earth. After fifteen hundred years, the designation is still both simple and profound. It was not until the middle of the Nineteenth Century that the making of the heavens and earth became the subject of a major controversy, still raging.

It is surely significant that the second most recurring question of the curious college student today concerns the topics of origins, cosmogony. Yet a student sincerely seeking an answer to his questions is hindered, not only by the unknowing scientist who misunderstands the teaching of the Christian chronicles, but even more so by the unknowing religionist who carelessly caricatures the Christian faith.

Not many scientists refuse the title of "Maker of Heaven and Earth" to the Supreme Being worship by so many. But most of them indignantly or sadly repudiate the scheme of things put forth by some worshipers. Here is a striking commentary on the situation prevailing today:

It often happens that a non-Christian derives from the clearest arguments, or from the evidence of his senses, certain scientific knowledge about the heavens and earth—about the size or distance or movements or revolutions of the stars, about certain eclipses of

the sun and moon, about the course of the seasons
and years, about the nature of animals and plants and
minerals, and other such things.

It is both improper and mischievous for any Christian man to speak on such matters as if so authorized
by Scripture and yet talk so foolishly that the unbeliever, observing the extravagance of his mistakes, is
scarcely able to keep from laughing. And the real
trouble is not so much that the man is laughed at for
his blunders, but that writers of Scripture are believed to have taught such things, and are thus con-
demned and rejected as ignorant by people outside
the Church, to the great loss of those whose salvation
we so much desire.

They find one belonging to the Christian body
so far wrong on a subject they themselves know so
well; and, on top of this, find him enforcing his
groundless opinions by the authority of our Holy
Bible. So they come to regard the Scriptures as un-
sound on subjects they have learned by observation
or by unquestioned evidence. Are they likely therefore to put their trust in these Scriptures about the
resurrection of the dead, the hope of eternal life, and
the kingdom of heaven?

What trouble and sorrow some presumptuous men
bring on their more careful brethren. When charged
with wrong notions by non-Christians, they try to
bolster their wrong assertions by the Bible, even
quoting inaccurately what they think will suit their
purpose and putting forth a lot of talk without understanding what they are saying.[1]

It surprises most people, hearing or reading the fore-
going paragraphs, to learn that they are as old as the

[1] From the Latin, *De Genesi ad Litteram*, Book I, Chapter xix, 39.

Apostles' Creed, having been written by Saint Augustine in the fourth century!

Apparently, the great Bishop of Hippo found his witness to intellectual pagans greatly hindered by some of his own side who were not content with the words of the Apostles' Creed or the majestic introduction of the Book of Genesis: "In the beginning God created the heavens and the earth." And today, the witness of concerned believers to intellectual pagans is likewise hindered by those who insist upon interpreting the Scriptures by the concepts of more than a century ago.

The result is that scientists, sympathetic and unsympathetic, gather the impression (as in the days of Augustine) that popular and old-fashioned fallacies are actually taught in Scripture. One has heard a modern man with a pre-Victorian mentality insist that the Scriptures teach the flat earth theory because a verse in the Prophecy of Isaiah speaks of "the four corners of the earth." His literal mind produced a quadrilateral from the literary style of a poetic utterance!

But the converse is also true. The certain fact that the best-known and best-loved translation of the Scriptures into the English tongue was made by literary geniuses who unavoidably shared the scientific concepts of four hundred years ago convinces some students that the Originals have set forth the same notions. Take, for example, the word "raqia" in the first chapter of Genesis translated by the King James Translators as a "firmament," clearly conveying their idea of a solid vault of heaven. The meaning of the Hebrew word "raqia" is expanse, for which no apology is needed in the space age.

The Christian student at a university may find six major theories of the beginnings of things competing for his intellectual assent. There are more than six schemes propounded, but there are at least six demanding attention:

1. (Pantheistic) Eternal Existence
2. (Atheistic) Spontaneous Evolution
3. (Theistic) Immediate Creation
4. (Deistic) Mediate Evolution
5. (Theistic) Restitutive Creation
6. (Theistic) Progressive Creation

The first two are impossible for a Christian intellectual; the second two are possible, but have opposite weaknesses; and the third two endeavor to harmonize the so-called conflict between the Scriptures and Science.

1. The Pantheistic Theory of Eternal Existence.

From the point of view of Scripture, the Pantheistic theory of the Eternal Existence of the Universe presented by Hinduism is impossible for Christians to accept, for it flatly denies that God created the heavens and the earth.

This theory from the point of view of Science likewise is difficult for a Christian to consider, for it contradicts the almost unanimous view of the universe held by scientists—that the universe had a beginning, suggested by many phenomena that allow calculation of the age of the universe. An isotope of uranium, for example, has a half life of 4,500,000,000 years. If the universe had existed from eternity, there would be today no accountable radioactive uranium, unless some processes utterly unknown produced it.

It is also recognized by scientists that there will be an end of all things. The Second Law of Thermodynamics suggests that the universe is running down, for, in the noted dictum of Clausius "Die Energie der Welt ist konstant, die Entropie strebt einem Maximum zu," the degradation of energy is implied, as is a beginning and end to our whole system.

On two counts, therefore, it is impossible for a Christian to accept the Pantheistic Theory of the External Existence of the Universe.

2. The Atheistic Theory of Spontaneous Evolution.

This theory plainly contradicts the Scripture which declares that in the beginning God created the heavens and the earth. And even if Scripture did not make such a categorical statement, this theory would be utterly impossible for a Christian whose whole faith is based on the concept of God.

The Christian student finds the theory difficult from utterly non-Scriptural arguments also. It postulates that the universe began by mere chance and an argument against chance has already been stated in the treatise "Chance and the Cosmos."

A good argument has been made that the agreed age of the earth does not permit enough time for the development of even a protein molecule, and although experiments with a theoretically reconstructed primitive atmosphere and electric arc have produced amino acids, it is a tremendous strain upon credulity to suppose that life with all its wonders came into being by blind chance.

I am reminded of a debate I had with the president of a rationalist society. The venue was the town hall, the chairman was the president of the local Rotary Club, and the topic was "That Faith in God is Most Reasonable." The chairman ruled that the challenger would lose the debate if he failed to show that faith in God was unreasonable or that his view—Chance—was more reasonable. Despite his brilliance, he inevitably failed.

3. The Theistic Theory of Immediate Creation.

The theory of an immediate creation by the Supreme Being is held by many sincere Christians today. It was held by many more Christians in the last generation, and by an even greater number among our grandparents. Therefore, unlike the previous two theories, one must conclude that this view is certainly possible for a Christian. Unfortunately, those who hold it insist upon too literal a view of Scriptural language, and too fallacious a view of scientific facts.

The theory in its most popular form is stated in the chronology of Archbishop Ussher, who concluded that the world was created 4004 B.C. A seventeenth century Cambridge scholar, Lightfoot, carried Ussher's conclusions further, and claimed that the Creation took place during the week of October 18-24, 4004 B.C., Adam being created at nine o'clock on the morning of October 23rd, Mesopotamian time (forty-five degrees east of Greenwich). As a scholar, commented a critic, Lightfoot the Hebrew professor was not prepared to commit himself any farther than that!

Of course, it is quite possible for a Christian to follow Archbishop Ussher's reasoning and add together the ages of the various patriarchs, arriving at the date 4004 B.C. The difficulty is that not all evangelical scholars agree that the pre-Abrahamic patriarchal names set forth in the Scriptures were of father-and-son. The New Testament permitted itself the latitude of calling the Lord Jesus Christ the son of David, the son of Abraham, which, taken literally, would mean that the Christ was a grandson of Abraham. The Old Testament likewise permitted itself latitude with the word "begat." Most Biblical scholars including many evangelical intellectuals, are inclined to regard the patriarchs named as heads of families or founding dynasts.

But when a Christian as a scientist studies the Grand Canyon of Arizona or the Giant's Causeway of Antrim, Ussher's dates become ludicrous. A Canadian can study Niagara and calculate the thousands of years that the River has been cutting back its gorge from Lake Ontario towards Lake Erie. A visitor to Yellowstone National Park can see clearly, at Specimen Ridge, that forest after forest has been bituminized between successive layers of rocks, going back a hundred thousand years. There are examples from every part of the whole wide world to be considered. Believers in Immediate Creation dated 4004 B.C. must also ignore the inexhaustible evidence of fossils in the rocks. Few would descend to the pathetic opinion of a brilliant naturalist, Philip Henry Gosse, who averred that God had placed these fossils in the rocks to test men's faith, a view which repelled his famous son, Sir Edmund Gosse, from adherence to evangelical faith.

4. The Deistic Theory of Mediate Evolution.

Deistic Mediate Evolution presupposes that the Divine Creator triggered the development of the Universe as well as initiated the process of evolving life. As such, this is more satisfactory than an atheistic or pantheistic view of evolution. Its chief weakness is that it runs counter to the scriptural revelation of God as active in the process of creation, and the objections to Deism on a previous page apply here too.

It should be said that some Biblical scholars* were confronted with a mass of evidence presented by advocates of evolutionary theory without the second thoughts of evolutionists themselves. Consequently, they were willing to go much farther to accommodate their convictions to views that have long since been modified. Scientists today are very ready to concede that new forms of life, reptiles, tortoises, mammals, appear in the geological record "suddenly." The picture-language of the first chapter of Genesis, as it is variously interpreted, suggests such novelties.

It could be said that those first accepting the Deistic Theory of Mediate Evolution too readily accommodated themselves to unconfirmed ideas and discounted too easily Scriptural revelation. They numbered faithful evangelical Christians—both then and now—among them, demonstrating that such views are not incompatible.

5. The Theistic Theory of Restitutive Creation.

There are two attempted harmonies of Scripture and Science to consider. The viewpoint so widely popularized in the Scofield Reference Bible accepts the evidences of evolution as all applying to a primitive creation, but teaches that, about four thousand years before Christ, God reconditioned the earth in six literal days. This attempted harmony concedes all the time necessary to produce the geological record. It inserts these ages between the first and second verses of the first chapter of Genesis, making it appear that God first created the heaven and the earth, as in verse one; then, as in verse two, He re-created it. From a Scriptural point of view, this argument for re-creation is made to depend upon translating the word "was" as "became."

There are two major objections to the Theory of Restitutive Creation. One is that it has no scientific backing. The other is that Scriptural support is very weak if not entirely lacking. Leading Hebrew scholars in the United Kingdom and the United States reject the translation of the Hebrew word "hayathah" as "became," on grounds of improper syntax. The accepted translation of Genesis, chapter one, verses 1 and 2 is:

> In the beginning God created the heavens and the earth. The earth was without form and void, and darkness was upon the face of the deep; . . .

6. *The Theistic Theory of Progressive Creation.*

Two of the theories previously considered have one thing in common, their theism. There remains another theistic theory, a harmony also of Scripture and Science, Progressive Creation.

The Progressive Creation school teaches that God brought the universe into being by successive actions of creation, as depicted logically in the first chapter of Genesis, each being followed by a lengthy period of evolutionary development. Of course, this view may be called Interrupted Evolution, but it differs from Deistic Mediate Evolution by allowing for the intervention of Divine power to bring about the major changes along the line of development. It might be described as a combination of Immediate Creation and Mediate Evolution.

This school provides a feasible interpretation of the statements of the first chapter of Genesis, treating it as a logical (rather than chronological) pictorial presentation of the beginnings of things. In contrast with the legends of the Babylonians and Egyptians, there is in

Genesis a majesty and simplicity and credibility of statement. Second, it embodies the proven facts of scientific observation, postulating the Divine Creator to explain the mystery of initial impulse and intermediate change as well as the regular development seen in the geologic records.

From this survey, it is apparent that a Christian student of science must categorically reject both the Pantheistic Theory of the External Existence of the Universe and the Atheistic Theory of Spontaneous Evolution.

The thinking Christian may embrace either Theistic Immediate Creation or Deistic Mediate Evolution, but in one case may have too fallacious a view of the findings of Science, and in the other too weak a view of Scriptural revelation.

A Christian may decide upon one of the many harmonies of Scripture and Science, the Theory of Restitutive Creation or the Theory of Progressive Creation, to name the two considered, frankly facing the problems involved.

Certainly, there is no ground for the conviction that a choice must be made between the atheistic dogmas of anti-Christians and the unscientific dogmas of unreasoning Christians.

Who has the final word in interpretation?

---

* It comes as a surprise to present-day fundamentalists that men such as B. B. Warfield and R. A. Torrey were willing to accept the theory of Deistic Mediate Evolution as possibly explaining the whole of animal creation except Man. The evangelical stalwarts, James Orr of Edinburgh, and Augustus Strong of Rochester, were both inclined to accept Deistic Evolution, within certain limits, as the Divine process of creation.

IV

THE REVELATION OF GOD

FAR-FLUNG ACROSS THE TWO MAIN ISLANDS of New Zealand are the huge towers and heavy lines of the hydro-electric system for which the country is justly famed. Throbbing along those lines is power at 220,000 volts to illuminate and energize remote farms and busy factories alike.

I have seen, far below those lines in the remote forests of the Waikaremoana, the huts of isolated Maori families still using primitive lamps for illumination. Those 220,000 volts of electricity were not so far away in terms of vertical distance. They could have wired their huts with the 220-volt equipment available in New Zealand. But the mighty, throbbing power of the hydro-electric system was not only far above their heads but actually beyond their utilization. They could not operate 220-volt equipment from a 220,000-volt line. A transformer was needed to step down the current to their lowly level of use.

So it is with Deity. Almighty God, Maker of heaven and earth, beyond man's comprehension, is to many famed philosophers not only a God unknown but One Unknowable. Mortal man needs a Transformer to step down the mighty power of Deity to levels of human comprehension. Needed once for all time is a revelation of God in man.

One man in history claimed to be that revelation of

God. The *Encyclopaedia Britannica* has devoted twenty thousand words to his biography. Arnold Toynbee in his monumental work has given more space to Jesus of Nazareth than to any other six great men, such as Buddha, Alexander, Cæsar, Mohammed, Napoleon and Lincoln.

An official propagandist of the anti-Christian government of Soviet Russia told me in Moscow that they regarded Jesus Christ as the greatest teacher of pre-modern times. Most thinking men will agree that the influence of Jesus Christ for good among men has been without rival.

Who was this remarkable Man? If His life had ended in scandal or disillusion, it would be well to study Him from points of view other than His own. But a perfect life demands respectful hearing of what He Himself claimed to be.

Jesus told Philip in the hearing of the apostles "He who has seen me has seen the Father."

The Apostle Paul quoted a hymn of the early Church in stating it thus in I Timothy iii, 16:

> He was manifested in the flesh,
> vindicated in the Spirit,
>   seen by angels,
> preached among the nations,
> believed on in the world,
>   taken up in glory.

It may be objected that when Jesus Christ said that one who had seen Him had seen the Father revealed, He must have meant something else. To this it must be said that, challenging a similar statement, his heresy-hunting countrymen cried: "We're not going to stone you for any good things, ... but for blasphemy: because you, who are only a man, are making yourself out to be God."[1] So on several occasions, He was threatened with death for making claims of Deity.

Jesus Christ boldly stated: "Truly, truly, I say to you, before Abraham was, I am." In the hearing of His disciples He prayed: "Father, glorify thou me . . . with the glory which I had with thee before the world was made."

His coming as Messiah was foretold by many Hebrew prophets, but His eternal agelessness (as the Incarnation of God in human form) was announced by the prophet Micah in speaking of the village of Bethlehem as the birthplace of the Messiah: ". . . from you shall come forth for me, one who is to be ruler in Israel, whose origin is from of old, from ancient days."

Thus the Eternal One, the Lord of all, Who had the "whole wide world in His hands," became incarnate in man . . . in the words of the carol:

> There's a tumult of joy
> O'er the wonderful birth,
> For the Virgin's sweet boy
> Is the Lord of the earth.

Thus it is that Christian people confess:

> I believe in God the Father Almighty . . . And in Jesus Christ, his only Son, our Lord . . .

There are some who believe that Jesus Christ was the Son of God in the sense that all humans are children of God—by God's ultimate creation. But there are statements in Scripture to emphasize the uniqueness of His Sonship—we are children (tekna) of God, but He is described in John i, 14 as the "only born" or "only begotten" (monogenous) of the Father.

[1] From *The New Testament in Modern English,* © J. B. Phillips 1958. Used with permission of the Macmillan Company. (John x, 33.)

It is difficult to illustrate a mystery so profound. A sculptor may take a block of granite, and may chisel the lifelikeness of a little boy from it. The statue may be exhibited in an art gallery as the work of his hands, the offspring of his mind. The same sculptor, by natural procreation, may beget a son, also in his likeness, but of the same substance—flesh, blood, bone and nerve—as the father. The statue of the boy, in human likeness, is the work of his hands, his creation; the person of the living boy, of the same substance and being, is begotten or born of him. We are made in the likeness of God, but created from the dust, and He is begotten of the Father, of "one substance"—eternal, holy, just, omnipotent, omniscient, omnipresent. Only-begotten (monogenous—properly "only born") does not refer to the birth of Jesus to Mary through the operation of the Holy Spirit, but to the eternal relationship of Son to Father.

To counteract erroneous notions about Jesus Christ, early Christians made their confession of Him most specific:

Who was conceived by the Holy Ghost, Born of the Virgin Mary . . .

The doctrine of the Virgin Birth of Jesus is clearly stated in the Gospel of Matthew and the Gospel of Luke. The argument that omission—the argument of silence—by the writers of Mark and John may discredit the other accounts of the Birth is truly a feeble one.

There are those who hold that the doctrine of the Virgin Birth of Christ is no more than a legend comparable to other legends of miraculous birth of other figures of antiquity. One has only to compare the dignified narrative of the Physician Luke with the fanciful language of the legend of the conception of Gautama Buddha.

That the "Holy Spirit will come upon you, and the power of the Most High will overshadow you" is far more credible of a first century man of science narrating what he was told by witnesses reporting an astounding happening.

The doctrine of the Deity of Christ is not based on the Virgin Birth. Rather it should be said that a believer in the Deity of Christ, so well-attested otherwise, may not find it a thing incredible to accept the miraculous birth of Jesus Christ.

Scientific arguments against the possibility or probability of human parthenogenesis or virgin birth are all arguments against the likelihood of such a thing occurring in ordinary society, not an argument against its occurrence once at the crossroads of history when Almighty God chose to appear among men.

The Apostles' Creed continues to specify:

Suffered under Pontius Pilate, Was crucified, dead, and buried: He descended into hell; The third day he rose again from the dead; He ascended into heaven, And sitteth on the right hand of God the Father Almighty: from thence he shall come to judge the quick and the dead.

As far as a Christian could, I traveled from the coast of the Hedjaz in Saudi Arabia towards the Holy Places of Islam. Mecca and Medina are forbidden to non-Moslems. In Medina, I would have wished to view Mohammed's tomb, for his bones are there, just as the bones of the Buddha are in India, and the corpse of Kung Fu-tze lies in China. In Jerusalem, I was shown an empty tomb, for it is assuredly believed among Christians that Jesus Christ rose from the dead.

Likewise, the doctrine of the Resurrection is not a legend which arose centuries later, but is based on the evidence of eyewitnesses, of whom there were hundreds. The Resurrection was an event unique in history, a promise of hope to all believers in the salvation of God.

The perfect life of Jesus Christ is the wonder of the ages. His was the sum of all human virtue. His was a freedom from all human sin. Yet He was perfectly human—He breathed, He walked, He talked, He hungered, He thirsted, He slept, He wept, and, when His human frame could bare no more in the crucifixion, He died.

His claims about Himself were astounding. He could have said that His was the work of showing humanity the way, explaining the truth, living the life —all of which a good teacher could have said. But He chose to say: "I am the way, and the truth, and the life; no one comes to the Father, but by me." And no other human could say that.

He said: "I am the light of the world." "I am the good shepherd." "I am the door; if any one enters by me, he will be saved." His influence transformed the lives of His disciples. His message through them first transformed a Mediterranean world which had produced "the glory that was Greece and the grandeur that was Rome." Their continuing enterprise so transformed the whole world, there is scarcely a place where the good influence of Christ has not been felt.

The message of Jesus emancipated womankind. From being a chattel of man, women became free and equal through the Good News proclaimed by Jesus Christ. Even in lands of other alien faiths polygamy has been abandoned through influence of the Gospel. In the name of Christ, numberless orphanages were founded, and child welfare was promoted—until it became the policy of the state.

Compassion of Christ for the sick energized His followers, who multiplied their hospitals and leprosaria and asylums, until again the modern state adopted the idea—and Christians continued their work by supplementing such official aid as well as extending medical help to under-privileged communities of alien and sometimes antagonistic faith and practice.

The compassion of Christ moved many of His followers to press for prison reform. The basic philosophy of Christ undermined the structure of slavery. The teaching call of Christ spurred His followers to promotion of education for all, an objective later adopted by the secular state, but still supplemented by Christians.

The Carpenter Who said: "Come to me, all who labor and are heavy-laden, and I will give you rest!" became the friend of the laboring man. "God," said Lord Shaftesbury, "has not ordained that in a Christian country there should be an overwhelming mass of foul, helpless poverty." So the workers affected by the social impact of the great Evangelical Awakenings today enjoy the highest standard of living of all time.

Yet Christians unite in declaring that all this material benefit is as nothing compared with the spiritual blessing of eternal life in Christ, and "this is eternal life, that they know thee the only true God, and Jesus Christ whom thou hast sent."

V

THE QUESTION OF AUTHORITY

ONE AMONG STUDENTS' recurring questions is:
"What is our authority for what we believe?"

"I'll tell you what I believe," a man once told me.
"If you do your best, God will do the rest."

"That's a very nice religion," I replied, "but what's your authority for believing it?"

"That's what I believe," he repeated. And he did not think it necessary to produce any authority.

In considering the question of authority from a Christian standpoint, one can afford to begin with a dogmatic statement. For the Christian, the supreme authority is Jesus Christ.

If a man says "I'm a Marxist, but I don't accept the authority of Karl Marx!" then he ought in all honesty to change his self-description somewhat. If a lady claims "I'm a vegetarian, but I mean by that—I eat the meat of vegetable-eaters!" then a less confusing word should be found.

Likewise, if a man says "I'm a Christian, but I don't accept the authority of Jesus Christ," then he ought to change his self-description to something else, a humanist, a democrat, or the like.

There are varied schools of authority throughout Christendom today—for example, the Roman Catholic, Greek Orthodox, and varied Protestant denominations. Without discussing denomination let us consider the various schools of thought in as simple a way as possible.

In Christendom, there are three main views of authority taught: there are those who believe in traditional authority: there are others who believe in rational authority: there are those who believe in evangelical authority. These terms, traditional, rational and evangelical authority, are deserving of explanation.

By traditional authority is meant the premise that the traditions which have been handed down from generation to generation constitute a vital court of appeal for dogma. By rational authority is meant the opinion that all religious beliefs or experiences must be finally attested by man's logical faculty. By evangelical authority is meant the view that Scripture itself is the final court of appeal in all matters concerning the Christian faith. Of course, traditionalists make use of both reason and gospel in establishing their doctrine and dogma, but grant overriding powers to the voice of tradition in the Church. Rationalists consider both tradition and gospel kindly, but override both with the conclusions of their own making in any given instance. And evangelicals by no means despise either tradition or logic, but use the Holy Scriptures as their final test of faith. Many people hold intermediate views and take no trouble to come to a final conclusion in the matter of religious authority.

1. Traditional Authority

On one occasion, I asked a friendly professor at a university maintained by a denomination of emphatic traditionalism:

"Why do you believe in purgatory?"

"That's the teaching of the Church," he replied.

"But what's your authority for so teaching?"

"It is a well-established tradition," said he.

"But," I protested, "I can't find anywhere in the New Testament, or in the writings of the Early Fathers, for that matter, any teaching about a doctrine of purgatory."

"No," he agreed. "But one mustn't think for a moment that all the truth of our religion has been written into the New Testament."

A discussion of the doctrine of limbo proceeded along very similar lines.

"Limbo," explained the kindly churchman, "is a kind of twilight heaven to which all unbaptized babies go, if they die young."

"Is it a kind of heaven?" I asked.

No—these infants could not see the face of God.

"Is it a kind of hell?" I inquired.

He explained that there is no punishment there.

"Then is it a kind of purgatory?" I persisted.

He affirmed that it was not a purgatory either, for there was neither suffering nor torment nor hope of release from the state of limbo.

"You see, Orr," he went on. "These infants, not being baptized, cannot go to heaven, and a merciful God could not send them to hell, so they go to the intermediate state of limbo."

And when I gently asked again for his authority for so believing, he again referred me to the teachings of his Church based on late traditions.

In 1954, it was my privilege to visit the beautiful Indian State of Kerala. One day, I was walking around a beautiful garden of tropical verdure, being accompanied by a Mar Thoma clergyman.

"What kind of a tree is this?" I asked my guide.

"That's a cashew nut tree," he explained.

I told him that I had often eaten cashew nuts, but had never previously seen the cashew nut tree. A very lovely tree it was.

"Tell me," I asked, "what is this thing on the top of the fruit?"

"That's the seed," he replied.

"Outside the fruit?" I queried.

When he told me that this was the case, I was amazed. He laughed and explained.

"In South India, among the Christians there is an old tradition that God did not make the cashew nut tree. They say that Moses made it!"

I begged him to tell me more.

"Moses," he continued with a chuckle, "went to the Lord and said: 'Lord, you have made everything. Why not let me make something?' And when the Lord asked Moses what he would like to make, Moses said he would like to make a tree. Of course, Moses wasn't acquainted with those verses that say 'Poems are made by fools like me, but only God can make a tree.' "

I was very amused by his story and its sequel.

"Moses," he continued, "studied other trees to see how they were made, and, after working on one for about seventeen years, finally produced a tree and brought it to the Lord for inspection. The Lord asked Moses: 'Where is the seed?' Alas, Moses had forgotten the seed. So, as an afterthought, he stuck the seed on top of the fruit like a candle on a cake!"

Much as I was entertained by that story, I did not accept it. Why? One cannot find any authority for it, either in the Books of Moses or the rest of the Old Testament or in the allusions to Moses in the New Testament. The tradition is neither scriptural nor reasonable.

In the Gospel of John, it is recorded that Jesus on the Cross saw His mother and the disciple he loved standing by, and He said to her: "Woman, behold your son!" To the disciple, John, He said: "Behold your mother!" From that hour, it is recorded, that disciple took her to his own home. Scripture is silent regarding her later life and demise, but there is nothing in the Scripture or the writings of the Fathers of the first three centuries to suggest that the destiny of Mary was different in kind to that of redeemed humanity. The story first appearing as disputed fiction in the fourth century suggested that the Blessed Virgin Mary was caught up into heaven. Adoration of Mary lent credibility to the tale. In the eighteenth century, a high Churchly Authority declared the tradition as not of sufficient worth to be set forth as a dogma, but in 1950 the tradition of the Assumption of the Blessed Virgin Mary bodily into heaven was proclaimed as an article of faith revealed by God and binding upon all.

There are traditions that are innocent in themselves. It would be more than difficult to prove that Jesus Christ was born on December 25th, the day commemorated as Christmas. It seems far more likely that He was born during the lambing season in Judæa, during April. But celebrating His birth in December is an old tradition, not yet made an article of faith by any hierarchy.

In London, it is customary to celebrate the birthday of Queen Elizabeth on the 10th of June. Actually, Her Majesty was born on the 21st of April, her father George VI on the 21st of December, yet it is customary to celebrate the British Monarch's birthday with parades and ceremonies in the month before midsummer. Anyone knowing anything of the British climate knows why. It does no harm to celebrate the royal birthday in June, but it would be a hardship on the conscience of an immigrant to one of the Queen's Dominions to insist that he believe that the Lady was actually born on June 10th, before granting voting rights.

2. *Rational Authority*

That brilliant statesman, Thomas Jefferson, compiled an abridgement of the Gospels known now as the Jefferson Bible, in which he included all the stories of Christ which appealed to his reason, and from which he excluded Christ's claims of deity and reported miracles. Thomas Jefferson was a deist, so he rejected the supernatural completely. It did not seem to matter to him that there were eyewitnesses of the miracles and resurrection of Christ. His own reason was the supreme authority for him. There was nothing that human intellect in general, and his mind in particular, could not understand.

This reminds me of a happening in England. A Methodist minister left for Annual Conference with the warnings of his wife ringing in his ears that he was working too hard, risking a breakdown. He promised her a quiet holiday away in Scotland as soon as the conference was over.

The man of God missed the last train to his home town, but caught a train to a neighboring town, and commenced a midnight hike five miles along the country lanes and roads. He was tired and his brain fevered, but the thought of their vacation in the Highlands lent him strength for the last few miles. It was a glorious moonlit night.

Suddenly, he heard what sounded like a lion's roar resound across the meadows. He started! He knew he must have imagined it, so he began walking again.

Again he heard the lion's roar, closer at hand. He stopped, his heart palpitating and his breathing quickened. He knew the lion's habitat was Africa, not England. He had been imagining things. His wife was right: he was near a nervous breakdown. So he began to walk forward again. Two minutes later, he heard a full throated roar, close at hand, so he stopped dead—scarcely daring to breathe. His imagination was still playing him tricks, of that he felt sure, yet that roar sounded so realistic! He waited. There seemed to be something—moving in the bushes up ahead. It was hard to visualize clearly in the moonlight. His eyes seemed to be fooling him as well as his ears, for he was sure he could see what looked like a lion with lashing tail upon the roadway up ahead. Mercifully, it showed no signs of attacking him. The minister backed away, then began to walk slowly with a fearsome backward glance until he reached a bend in the road, when he broke into a wild race for the station.

He took the milk train back to London. His mind was in a whirl. He must not alarm his wife or startle his colleagues, so he sent a telegram telling the good woman of the parsonage that he was unavoidably delayed. He checked in at a big Strand hotel, took a sleeping tablet and slept for twenty-four hours straight. On waking, he hoped that the encounter on the quiet country road would prove to be only a nightmare of his tired mind; but he could not shake off the impression that he had heard and seen an African lion in England.

Of course, his intellect told him that what he had seen was impossible. Whoever had seen a lion at large in England? In a zoo, yes; near a zoo, maybe: but not out in the countryside. There seemed nothing else to do but make an appointment with a psychiatrist—

perhaps, without involving his own name he could secure the name of a Christian psychiatrist from headquarters, one who would remember that Methodist parsons cannot afford to have nervous breakdowns.

Someone pushed a copy of the morning paper under the door. His eye was caught by a headline. All the animals which had escaped from the train wreck in the Midlands had been recaptured, it said. That explained everything—yet he had to admit that his reason had refused to believe the evidence of reliable ears and eyes.

It is obvious that people today do not witness miracles such as the feeding of the five thousand or the raising of the dead. It is often overlooked by the skeptics, however, that Christians do not claim that such happenings in catering or undertaking are to be expected in everyday life. It is confidently believed by Christians that the life of Christ represented a supernatural intrusion of Deity into the life of mankind. No scientist alive can assert that the miracles of Christ did not in fact happen. He can say such are unknown to him.

If human reason looks to Science to examine the facts of Christian faith, it runs into insuperable difficulty at the very beginning—the existence of God. What test could Science use? Barometer, or photoelectric cell, or Geiger counter?

If human reason depends on its own integrity as judge, it must be pointed out that Sin, the prime charge of the Christian faith against the human race, is capable of warping human judgment. I knew a fellow in Illinois who could tell a lie and repeat it so often that he finally believed it himself. Sin warped his judgment. And I met a fellow in the Philippines during the war (a gentleman by Act of Congress only, as we said) who

was living in a shack up the beach with a Filipina girl.
I said, as I saw him writing to his wife:

"I don't know how you do it!"

"Do what?" he asked.

"Write love letters to your wife while you shack up
the beach with this girl friend of yours!"

"I don't like your attitude," he said, darkly.

"My attitude!" I retorted.

"Yes, your attitude. My affair with Dolores is a true
friendship. I am ten thousand miles or more from
home: I have emotional needs."

"Scripture as well as Law calls it adultery!"

He was compelled to rationalize. He could not depend on his reason because of degrading sin. Sin in
mind is not the best judge of religious truth.

3. Evangelical Authority

The word Gospel is the Anglo-Saxon form of the
Greek word "euangelion" (evangel) that means simply
"good news." Evangelical authority may be explained
in a very few words: If anyone wishes to know what
Jesus Christ said and did, let him read the Gospels, the
good news, which record Christ's life and teaching.
By extension, the Epistles derived from the same
apostolic authority are included, and also the Acts and
the Revelation of John. The Gospels tell the story of
Jesus Christ, the Epistles are "letters to young churches"
interpreting Christ's message, and the whole of the New
Testament is derived, directly or indirectly, from those
who were eyewitnesses and ministers of the message.
By further extension, the Writings of the Old Testament are included in the authority of the evangelical,
who adopts the attitude of Christ and His apostles to-
ward the Hebrew Scriptures.

An evangelical is not scornful of traditions, unless contradicted by the letter or spirit of the Scriptures. An evangelical is happy to use the clear findings of science (whether geographical, archæological, biological, or philological) and the best thought of philosophy to help him understand the Scriptures. The Scriptures themselves remain for him the final authority in Christian faith. This subject we shall explore in detail.

VI

THE SCRIPTURES OF TRUTH

"THE FIRST," SAID JOHN QUINCY ADAMS, "and almost the only book deserving of universal attention is the Bible. I speak as a man of the world to men of the world, and I say to you, 'Search the Scriptures.'"

The Bible is not only a book of divine revelation, it is also a book of literary grandeur, sublime influence, human interest, amazing accuracy, perfect unity, and everlasting challenge.

We first consider the Gospels, the good news of Jesus Christ, because they tell the story of His life and teachings. The Gospels of Matthew, Mark, Luke and John are four accounts written from four different points of view — Matthew's Gospel written from a Jewish point of view and Luke's Gospel from a Greek point of view, with Mark's Gospel telescopic, John's retrospective.

Some may think that it is a weakness to have four different stories. Actually, it is a strength. If someone were to take another to court and sue for damages, producing four witnesses who told identical stories of how some accident occurred, the judge would throw the case out of court upon grounds of obvious collusion. In a street accident, a policeman sees things from a different point of view to the bus driver; and a passerby sees it quite differently than the pedestrian unfortunately knocked down.

The Gospels were compiled from the stories of eyewitnesses, written by those who witnessed events or those who interviewed such witnesses. If asked—Was Jesus Christ really transfigured on the mountain?—Peter and James and John could affirm that they had so seen Him. The authority lay in these Apostles. And the same witnesses and their associates wrote the Epistles, letters to newly founded churches, explaining difficult doctrine, correcting wrong ideas. The New Testament includes also the Acts of the Apostles and the Revelation of John, vastly differing books by apostolic writers.

The evangelical school of thought teaches that the final court of appeal regarding the life and teachings of Jesus Christ rests in the New Testament. In fact, apart from New Testament authors, people would know very little about Jesus Christ, for contemporary historians dismiss Him with a sentence or a paragraph.

A student at California Institute of Technology once challenged me thus:

"Sir, is it not a fact that there is a Gospel of Thomas and a Gospel of Peter? Why were such writings omitted from the New Testament?"

I added that not only were spurious books omitted, but that good books such as the *Shepherd of Hermas* and the *Teaching of the Twelve Apostles* were also omitted, for the simple reason that they were not considered apostolic writings.

"Is it not a fact," he asked again, "that three hundred years or so after Christ the Church decided which books should be included in the New Testament?"

When I agreed that this was the case, quickly he suggested that such a procedure proved that the ultimate authority lay not in the Scriptures but in the Church continuing. From a conclusion such as this, I dissented strongly.

"The liberties and rights of the people of the United States," I said, "are chartered in the Constitution. The Supreme Court interprets the Constitution. Authority does not rest in the Supreme Court, but in the words of the Founding Fathers, ignoring for the moment the amendments added following the directions of the Founding Fathers. The authority of the New Testament is greater than the authority of the later churchmen, for the authority of the New Testament is based upon the testimony of actual witnesses."

"Supposing," said I, "World War III destroyed civilization as we know it. After the year 2000, the children of the survivors emerged from the caves and decided to reconstitute civilization as they had heard about it from their parents. So they appointed a committee on law, a committee on education, a committee on politics, a committee on commerce, and a committee on religion. The committee on religion decided that the first business was to collect the sacred writings of the Christian faith, the widest-spread religion.

"One man reported that he had found a book in the ruins of Los Angeles, the front pages burned, but the remainder indicating that it was a life of Jesus Christ and related material. Another man reported that he had found a book in the ruins of London, back pages burned, but the title clearly stating that it was the New Testament of the Lord and Savior Jesus Christ. Other copies in other languages were produced.

"Another researcher produced a copy of the Old Testament, and yet another the Old and New Testaments together. An enthusiastic youngster announced that he had found a missing book of the Bible, one entitled *The Robe,* by a prophet named Lloyd Douglas. Another wished to add *Science and Health* by a prophetess named Mary Baker Eddy. Another proposed for inclusion in the Bible *The Book of Mormon* by Joseph Smith. What method would the committee use to determine whether or not these books were what they were supposed to be, eyewitnesses' accounts of the life and teachings of Jesus Christ?

"The historical method could soon be applied. They could ascertain that *The Robe* had not been known before 1925, that *Science and Health* had not been known before 1875, and that *The Book of Mormon* was unknown to the press in 1825. The committee could decide that these books be read for what they are worth, but not that they were authentic apostolic writings.

"This was one of the methods employed by the Early Fathers in settling a New Testament canon. The sum-total of the accepted New Testament is quoted in writings of the earliest Church Fathers, with the exception of eight verses of the Gospel of John. A cross reference of such writings shows that the Gospels and Epistles were accepted by the Early Church, and that the rejected writings were rejected after careful study."

The Old Testament is an unfolding revelation of God whereas the New Testament is a final revelation of God. This does not mean that the Old Testament is not inspired. Rather it means that while the Old Testament has been superseded in certain points as a revelation of God's will, the New Testament has never been surpassed.

In many Mohammedan countries, any citizen who has lost interest in his wife need only to clap his hands three times and say before witnesses "I divorce thee!" The woman has no recourse, but is compelled to return to her father's household. This was the practice of some Jews in the days of Christ. But the Master hated the system, and told his countryman that this license had been allowed them by Moses because of the hardness of their hearts. So He clearly stated the rules of Christian marriage which are infinitely superior to the interpretations of Moses.

In the case of the law of retaliation, it was the same. The Law said: ". . . eye for eye, tooth for tooth." But Jesus Christ superseded that with the commandment to love one's enemies. New Testament standards were unsurpassed and final. Why? Because Jesus Christ was the final revelation of God, unsurpassed, unique.

What should one's attitude be to the Old Testament? For a Christian, the first example is Jesus Christ Himself. He quoted it as having fullest authority. He said, "It is written, Man shall not live by bread alone . . ." and His quotations demonstrated His reliance on Scripture. The canonical Old Testament Scriptures were recognized by the Hebrew rabbis, just as the canonical New Testament Scriptures were recognized by Christians. The Jews did not acknowledge the authority of the Apocryphal Books, nor do Protestants.

All of Christendom is united in considering the sixty-six books of the Old and New Testaments authentic. Some denominations add to their list the disputed books of the Apocrypha.

Most Christians profess to believe that the Old and New Testaments are inspired, but there is by no means agreement upon what constitutes inspiration. The New Testament itself contains a definite statement on inspiration: "All scripture *is* given by inspiration of God and *is* profitable for doctrine, for reproof, for correction, for instruction in righteousness: That the man of God may be perfect, thoroughly furnished unto all good works."[1] (The American Revised Version of 1901 translates the phrase "Every scripture inspired of God

[1] II Timothy iii, 16, 17.

is . . . profitable . . ." but the American Revised Standard Version of 1952 returns to the sense of the Authorized Version of 1611 in stating "All scripture is inspired by God . . .")

Inspiration is a word of Latin derivation. The Greek word essentially means "God-breathed." It was my privilege to address the student body of Gordon College in Boston. A foreign student stood to his feet to ask: "May I say a word? The oldest translation of the Bible into a vernacular language is the Armenian. I come from Armenia in Asia Minor. It is interesting that the title of the Armenian Bible was taken from a Bible text, from the verse which is translated in English 'All scripture is inspired . . .' Consequently, the Armenian translators called their Scriptures 'Asdwadza Shoonch'—'The Breath of God!'"

So the Scripture itself claims that all Scripture is "God-breathed." But what does it mean to be "God-breathed" or "inspired"? No one knows. The Scriptures themselves say only that "men moved by the Holy Spirit spoke from God." The Scriptures declare that God breathed into man's nostrils the breath of life and he became a living soul. No one knows by what method God breathed into the nostrils of man, but everyone—as did the first avowed agnostic, Thomas Huxley—can see that between Man and the higher mammals there "is a great gulf, a divergence immeasurable, practically infinite." Likewise as a result of God-breathing into the Holy Scriptures, there is a divergence immeasurable between the Bible and non-Biblical literature.

One of our planes crashed at Westover Field in Massachusetts (at which I was Base Chaplain) and it was my sad duty to go to the girl who had lost her husband in that crash to break the news of her husband's death.

Her father had died five months before, her mother had died at her birth, and her husband had been "all she possessed." She wept, and, as I wanted to comfort her, I began to read the 23rd Psalm—till I came to the phrase: "Even though I walk through the valley of the shadow of death, I will fear no evil; for thou art with me; . . ." and she was comforted. Why did I not read a line from Omar Khayyam, or William Shakespeare? No, I know the transforming power of Scripture.

One of my friends who described himself as a modernist told me very cheerfully, "Of course, I believe that the Bible is inspired—it inspires me, so I know that it is inspired." That amused me. By the same token, one could say that Shakespeare was inspired, Kipling inspired, Longfellow inspired, and practically anyone whose writings appealed to anyone! That is not what is meant by Inspiration where Scripture is concerned.

On the other hand, one of my friends who was an extreme fundamentalist told me that he believed that every word, from cover to cover, of the Authorized Version was inspired. I thought he was being rhetorically extravagant until I found that he really did believe in the inspiration of the Committee appointed by King James, for he included the Dedication to His Majesty, as well as the chapter headings. His was a rare case!

One of the theories popular among extreme fundamentalists is a kind of verbal dictation theory—that God dictated each word to His prophets and apostles the way one dictates to one's stenographer. Not many real evangelicals (certainly not educated evangelicals) hold such a position.

In his Letter to the Corinthians, the Apostle Paul complains about the divisions in the church at Corinth. He says, "I am thankful that I baptized none of you, except Crispus and Gaius;" and follows with the explanation, "lest any one should say that you were baptized in my name." Having another thought, Paul added: "I did baptize also the household of Stephanas." And as a final afterthought he stated: "Beyond that, I do not know whether I baptized any one else." It is obvious from this paragraph that the Apostle was allowed the latitude of his memory, and that the actual words were not dictated to him, consciously or unconsciously. Does that mean this passage was not inspired? By no means.

What then is the purpose of inspiration? The Scripture itself is explicit. It is profitable for doctrine, reproof, correction and instruction in righteousness. It is not meant to be a textbook of chemistry, physics, mathematics, geology, biology, or the like—though, allowing for pictorial language, it is free of the glaring scientific errors of its contemporaries in religious literature.

In Scripture is the claim that inspiration is both dynamic and plenary. But not only is it a literary disclosure of God, it is also a literary work of man, with human manifestations aplenty. The Holy Spirit allowed the sacred writers their own styles, figures of speech, symbols, and the like, and Scripture contains personification, history, poetry, drama, proverb, allegory and other fine literary devices which by no means conform to the exact language of law or science, though the latter also is evidenced. The Bible is a collection of human books, God inspired.

The human style of the writers of Scripture is clearly seen by anyone who can detach himself from the sixteenth century style of the English translators in the Authorized Version. I have a sister-in-law who is an abbreviationist—she contracts everything, possible and impossible. My wife has a sister-in-law who is a protractionist—she takes twenty minutes to describe what anyone else could do in five. Everyone has his own style. The Apostle Paul, for example, is prone to make a statement, insert a parenthesis, add a footnote, return to the statement, adjoin an explanation—just like a university professor! No wonder the Apostle Peter, a fisherman lacking the academic background of his confrere, said of his epistles, "There are some things in them hard to understand."

Figures of speech are permitted in the Sacred Writings. I heard a man describe a vacation he spent in the Hudson Bay country, where insects multiply in the muskeg. He said that he was bitten one hundred thousand times. His exaggeration was not deceitful—it was hyperbole, a recognized literary device. And hyperbole is employed in the Scriptures. The Gospels declare that John the Baptist appeared in a wilderness preaching, and all the country of Judæa and all the people of Jerusalem went out to him—all? Every man, woman, youth, maiden, boy, girl, baby and babysitter? No, not "all" in that sense. The word "all" is used in the same sense that one today uses the expression "Everybody is talking about him!"

Symbols occur plentifully in Scriptures, especially in apocalyptic writings. The Revelation of John declared that out of the mouth of Christ issued a two-edged sword—a statement obviously not to be taken literally. Jehovah's Witnesses seemed fascinated by the mention of the 144,000 in the same symbolical book. In fact, until a few years ago, when their membership passed that figure, they claimed that they were the predicted 144,000! And what is the symbolism of 144,000? Twelve is the number of perfection and a thousand the number of multitude, which interprets this number as "a perfectly-perfect multitude."

It is difficult to define the nature of the inspiration of

Scripture as there are at least a half dozen varieties.

a. There appears to be direct Revelation, in which Almighty God has spoken concisely to men, as in the case of the giving of the Law to Moses: "And God spoke all these words . . ."

b. There is likewise Revelation with Inspiration, as in the instance of the Lord speaking to John the Divine: ". . . write what you see, what is and what is to take place hereafter." This was not stenographic dictation.

c. In the Introduction to the Gospel of Luke is found Inspiration without Revelation: "Inasmuch as many have undertaken to compile a narrative of the things which have been accomplished among us, just as they were delivered to us by those who from the beginning were eyewitnesses and ministers of the word, it seemed good to me also, having followed all things closely for some time past, to write an orderly account for you, most excellent Theophilus, that you may know the truth concerning the things of which you have been informed." The text indicates that Luke collected and arranged his material in the best of journalistic style from reliable eyewitnesses.

d. There are occasional passages in Scripture where the source of the material is stated to be solely Inward Illumination. For example, in I Cor., vii, the Apostle Paul offers good advice on the subject of marriage: "Now concerning the unmarried, I have no command of the Lord, but I give my opinion as one who by the Lord's mercy is trustworthy. I think that in view of the impending distress it is well for a person to remain as he is." He gives other advice to married people, and likewise qualifies it: "I say this by way of concession, not of command."

e. Evident is Inspiration with Illumination, in a declaration of Paul the Apostle: "And we impart this in words not taught by human wisdom but taught by the Spirit, interpreting spiritual truths to those who possess the Spirit."

f. According to the writer himself, there is demonstrated Inspiration without Illumination. The Apostle Peter, writing of the Old Testament prophets, declared: "They inquired what person or time was indicated by the Spirit of Christ within them when predicting the sufferings of Christ and the subsequent glory. It was revealed to them that they were serving not themselves but you . . ." In other words, the prophets who predicted the sufferings and glory of Christ had no idea Who their Messiah would be. They wrote as men who were inspired in their hearts but by no means fully enlightened in their minds.

In view of the variety of inspiration noted in Scripture, it is very difficult to try to make the Scriptures fit a particular theory—rather it is wiser to make the various theories fit the pattern of the Scriptures.

A Church of England article of Holy Scripture is very appropriate: "Holy Scripture contains all things necessary to our salvation." We have a sure authority for our faith in the Old and New Testaments of the Holy Bible. But, is it wise to say that the Scriptures alone are the all-sufficient guide? Anyone who has ever discussed religion with a cultist knows that these determined folk are ready and willing to quote the Word of Scripture, particularly verses that can be wrested to suit their arguments. Jehovah's Witnesses quote texts to disprove the Deity of Christ, and the Deity of the Holy Spirit. No, it is not enough to rely on Scripture alone. A believer needs the Interpreter of Scripture, the Paraclete promised by Christ to guide him into all truth. The One Who inspired is the One Who alone can interpret.

I am reminded of an incident of student evangelism.

I was walking along the corridor of a dormitory in Seattle Pacific College. I heard a group of students having an argument, so I stopped to listen. (I did not mean to eavesdrop—I just wanted to hear what they were saying!)

"Listen, Joe," said one, "I'll tell you what Orr teaches on Sanctification." And he told it with a very Methodist flavor.

"Just a minute, Jim," said another, "I've heard Orr five times too, and I'll tell you just what he teaches on Sanctification." And he told it with a very Presbyterian flavor.

We heard the voice of authority—a sophomore.

"Pipe down everybody. I'll tell you what Orr teaches on Sanctification."

His exposition showed that he was, in air force slang, "totally off the beam." So I thought it was time for me to intervene.

"Good evening, men," I said. I was greeted by a chorus of voices telling me that they had just been talking about my lectures, and they wanted me to settle an argument. Asked a spokesman:

"What is meant in your book, *Full Surrender,* by positional, critical and progressive sanctification?"

I told them that it would take a few minutes; they urged me on. So I explained what I meant by positional, critical and progressive sanctification. The Methodist was satisfied. The Presbyterian was satisfied. But the sophomore never.

"Are you sure you meant that, Dr. Orr?"

"I'm sure," I replied.

"Are you sure you are sure?" he persisted.

"Well," I assured him, "I'm certain!"

He turned to the crowd of students.

"Listen, Jim, you've had your say, and, Joe, you've

had your say, and Dr. Orr has been kind enough to explain his thoughts on the matter. But allow me to have my say, and explain to you what I think that Dr. Orr must have meant when he wrote that book!"

We were all amused, for every author surely ought to know what he has meant in his writings. And the Author of Scripture, Who inspired Moses and David and Paul and the others, surely knows how to interpret the Word to those whose hearts He indwells.

The supreme authority for the Christian is the Lord Jesus Christ, and the vehicle of authority is the Holy Scriptures of the Christian faith, as interpreted by the Holy Spirit of God, to every trusting believer.

VII

THE PROBLEM OF SINNING

IN THE SABI RIVER COUNTRY, on the low veld of southeastern Africa, I heard the lions roar as they made the kill. It was a cruel business, but there was little that anyone could do about it—lions are beasts of prey, as nature intended. On any farm, one can hear the pigs grunt as they eat the garbage—pigs are scavengers, likewise as nature intended.

But could anyone say that Almighty God intended the human race to lie and to lust, to kill and to steal? There is something obviously wrong with human nature.

In 1937, Professor C. E. M. Joad held the chair of philosophy in the University of London. He was such a witty enemy of Christianity that a Rector of the Church of England there preached a sermon on "God, the Devil and Professor C. E. M. Joad!" Professor Joad held that there was nothing wrong with human nature that better education, better opportunity and better environment could not cure. He laughed at the problem of sin.

Came World War II to desolate half of Europe. The blitz brought the war to Dr. Joad's own doorstep and refugees revolted his righteous soul with their authenticated stories of the concentration camps. He revised his judgment.

Professor Joad changed his mind completely. What,

thought he, is history but the record of the follies of mankind, man's inhumanity to man. Dr. Joad decided that the theologians had a far deeper insight into human nature than that of contemporary Science. The doctrine of original Sin began to make sense to his mind.

Cyril E. M. Joad went further than that, and followed his arguments to a logical conclusion—he next embraced the Christian faith and was received into the Church of England that he had affected to despise. He died in the faith.

World War II certainly changed the thinking of many people. The resurgence of barbarism in a century boastful of its civilization exposed the exceeding sinfulness of humanity.

But this discovery of the Twentieth Century is nothing new to the Christian. The Christian knows by revelation and observation that "all have sinned and come short of the glory of God."

The Christian is able to go one step further and proclaim that "the wages of sin is death."

Mrs. Eleanor Roosevelt wrote to us while I was serving as base chaplain at Westover Air Base, during the War. She informed us that a good neighbor of hers at Hyde Park, a fine young fellow, seemed to be in trouble in the Service most of the time, and this she could not understand, for he had been such a fine lad in civilian life. Would we look into it?

I visited the young serviceman in the Base guardhouse. He was serving his third six-month sentence, following penalties which had become progressively heavy with the repetition of his offense. All that the President's Lady had said about him was true and it was just as true of most aspects of his military apprenticeship. He was a good soldier, had real initiative, carried out orders intelligently, was a first-rate shot, was healthy in body and clean in mind. He had, however, one little fault which marred his near-perfect record. Every time he was granted a weekend pass from the post, he did not show up again on time or voluntarily. Hence he was held in the guardhouse, and was finally discharged from the service. He begged me to get him shipped overseas to North Africa, where, he assured me he would not go absent-without-leave. The Base Commander agreed with this contention in all sympathy, but told me that he dare not send a disobedient soldier overseas. He must take his punishment. And so he went back to the farm that he loved, a sadder and wiser man.

In Brisbane, Queensland, when a teen-age craze for playing "chicken" with cars reached Australia, a crazy youngster drove his jalopy on the wrong side of the street, daring legitimate drivers to hold their lawful courses. A driver was killed outright, leaving four little children fatherless. The foolish one was held accountable.

What is true of military law and traffic law is true of nature's laws and the laws of society. The transgression of the law is punishable. And this principle obviously holds good for the moral law also, as a study of the problem, individually or collectively, will show.

The man who climbs the City Hall and jumps off may think that he defying the law of gravity. In a matter of seconds, he suffers for his silly defiance. The criminal who defies the moral law and thinks that he is getting away with it also suffers, here and hereafter.

Everyone therefore faces the problem of the guilt of sin. The problem of the ages is simply: How can a man be right with God?

A cowboy actor approached me at the Hollywood Christian Group with a straightforward question:

"How does God forgive sin?"

I quoted the Scripture in reply:

"In him we have redemption through his blood, the forgiveness of our trespasses . . ."

"What you mean," he retorted, "is that Jesus died for me! Now, I've heard that since I was a kid in Sunday School, but I don't believe it because I don't understand it."

I asked him to explain.

"Look, man," he replied. "The State of California is holding this fellow Chessman for capital punishment. Supposing I feel sorry for the fellow and ask the Governor to let me take his place in the gas chamber—would they let me take his place? No, they wouldn't. They would tell me, 'you did not commit the crime so we cannot let you take the punishment, no matter how much you feel sorry for him.' It would not be right. Now, that's why I don't understand what you call the atonement. It would not be right . . ."

"Frankly," said I, "the doctrine of the atonement is one of the most difficult to understand. I do not know that I can explain it satisfactorily, but perhaps I can illustrate by analogy."

When I was a boy in Ireland, I told him, I used to play ball out back. Diagonally across the lot from our house was the house of a resident called Albert Mann. His house was in the way, and every time we hit the ball hard, we were sure to break one of his windows.

One day, Mr. Mann rushed out of his house, shook his fist at us kids, and told us that the next brat to break his window would receive a broken ear! Who happened to be the next brat to break his window? I did not stop running until I reached home, but my longer-legged sister got home first, and informed my mother of my misdemeanor. That I did not mind—I could manage mother—but my father happened to be in the kitchen; he should have been in his shop. Under the circumstances I decided to retreat from the kitchen and seek a little more recreation elsewhere in the neighborhood.

My father grabbed me by the wrist. "You're coming with me, young man!" he said. I protested that the man would hit me, but my father soon propelled me to the door of the indignant Albert Mann. "Here's the boy that broke your window!" he announced.

Mr. Mann did not waste much time with me.

"Mr. Orr," he said, "I know that kids can't help breaking windows. I broke windows when I was a boy. But why is it that every time there is any window broken in this neighborhood, it has to be my window?"

I could have told him. His house was in the way. The consensus among the children was that Mr. Mann should emigrate to New Zealand!

"Mr. Orr," went on our neighbor, "I'm willing to forgive the boys. But I've had to fix eleven windows around this house this summer already. I'm willing to forgive the boys—but somebody has got to pay for it! Somebody has got to pay for it! Somebody has got to pay for it!"

My father paid for it, and (I told my inquirer) I had learned the first principle of forgiveness—when one is forgiven, someone must pay!

That was why there was a cross of atonement. But why Jesus Christ to die on that cross? Why not Moses or Joshua, Elijah or Ezekiel, Peter or Paul? I gave him another illustration.

Twenty years after the incident of the broken window, my sister's husband "borrowed" some money from me. There are different marriage customs in different countries. A Zulu in Africa will save up enough money to buy a wife. A Tamil in India will pay someone for taking one away. But, in my native Ireland, as soon as a man marries one's sister, he feels entitled to apply for a loan. So my brother-in-law borrowed one hundred pounds ($500 in those days) from me.

He promised to pay me back twenty shillings ($5) a week for two years, but, as he was my brother-in-law, I excused him from paying on Easter Week and Christmas Week. Alas, he never paid a penny back.

I bore him a grudge for a couple of years. Then I forgave him. But which of the two of us suffered? The sinner or the sinned against? I could have taken him to Court, had an injunction against him, and seized his furniture: then he would have suffered. But the moment I forgave him, I suffered—and that taught me the second principle of forgiveness: the one who forgives is the one who suffers. This is true to experience.

The only one able to forgive our sin is God. No one else could suffer for us. It was necessary for Almighty God to become Incarnate in Christ, and to suffer on the Cross for us.

There are many theories of the Atonement—the moral influence theory, the identification theory, and others. The substitution theory is the theory insisted upon by many ardent believers—that Christ died in our stead. This should not mean that Almighty God looked around and picked Jesus the son of Mary to die for humanity. No. Rather it means that God Himself chose to suffer for the sins of the world, and did so in the person of the Lord Jesus Christ, in whom we have redemption through His blood, the forgiveness of our sins, according to the riches of His grace.

"Therefore, being justified by faith, we have peace with God, through our Lord Jesus Christ." To be justified means "to be set right." That is the privilege of the believer.

VIII

THE PROBLEM OF LIVING

MY FRIEND, THE COWBOY ACTOR, listened well to the explanation about the forgiveness of sin. He seemed to grasp its implications. Then he shook his head and said:

"Not much good for me to ask God to forgive my sins. I would be doing the same things again next week!"

"Cheer up," said I. "There is an answer for that problem too—the problem of living."

Chaplain Wyeth Willard, the much decorated Marine, rushed me to Boston South Station to catch a train bound for Concord, New Hampshire. Alas, I missed the train, and found that the next one was much too late for my purpose. So I called the pastor of the church in Concord, and said:

"I've missed my train. The next one does not get me to Concord until eight-forty-five—can you keep the people singing from seven-thirty until quarter to nine?"

"That's no good," he replied.

"Shall we cancel the meeting then?" I asked.

"Oh, no!" he objected. "We have advertised you very widely, and we must keep faith with the folk. Where are you speaking from?"

"Boston South Station," I explained.

"Take a taxi to Logan Airport," he said, "and wait

at the Eastern Air Lines counter. One of my deacons is a reserve pilot, and he has his own light plane. He'll fly down to pick you up."

In due course, a youngish fellow in blue jeans approached the counter.

"Are you Edwin Orr?" he asked.

I identified myself.

"Missed your train?" he asked.

I nodded. "I'm sorry."

"Well, I missed my supper," he said. "But never mind. You ever flown before?"

"Thousands of hours!"

"Where was this?"

"Thirteenth Air Force in the Pacific," I said.

"Say, were you at Morotai?"

"Yeah," said I.

"Noemfoor? Biak?"

I agreed, and he told me that he had been a pilot with the Fifth Air Force, our neighbors.

We walked to the plane together, the pilot being obviously pleased to have a former comrade in arms alongside. The plane was a two-seater, dual controlled craft. The pilot placed me in the front seat, in the plexiglass bubble, and he sat one seat back, higher up. We took off.

When we reached about three thousand feet, I suddenly discovered that the pilot had misunderstood me. He took out his supper, began to open his ham sandwiches, and then said:

"Well, if you don't mind—I'll eat my supper, and you can fly the plane the rest of the way!"

When I had said that I had flown thousands of hours, I meant as a passenger, not as a pilot. I hated to disappoint him, and I saw a chance of learning to fly myself. I took over the controls.

I advanced the throttle, then retarded it. Then I depressed the pedals, first right, then the left: I banked the machine to the right and the left. I was learning fast.

"What do you think of her?" asked the pilot.

"Flies like a bird," I replied. But I did not tell him that I was having difficulty. The plane was continuing to rise, and I could not find out how to level it off. I had watched DC 3 pilots during the war push the joy stick away from them and pull it towards them, to descend or ascend. But this steering column, on which a half-moon wheel was mounted seemed to be fixed. I could not ask for advice without betraying my inexperience.

"What height are you gonna fly at?" said he.

"What height do you recommend?" I asked.

"You're supposed to fly at three thousand, five thousand, seven thousand or nine thousand going north." said he. "Eight thousand, six thousand, four thousand or two thousand south."

I would willingly have settled for any altitude. The plane continued to ascend. I felt up and down the column for a hidden locking device.

There was none. At long last, I hit upon the answer to the problem. The steering wheel was mounted on a rod which moved in and out of the steering column like an arm in a sleeve. I leveled off immediately. I was flying!

Flying gave me a new sense of power. The pilot interrupted my reverie.

"Where are you headed?"

"Which way am I supposed to head?" I asked.

"You see that light?" asked the pilot.

Light, I thought. The darkened landscape glittered with twinkling lights by the thousand.

"What light?" I asked.

"Look! Over there! Every minute on the minute. Dash and three dots! There it is!"

I saw the beacon (Lawrence, Massachusetts) and headed in that direction. When I asked the pilot for the next beacon, he told me that he would tell me in good time. He continued to help me, warning me when I was going to high or too low, or off compass direction. I suddenly realized that I had a good co-pilot alongside.

After we passed Manchester, New Hampshire I started to feel uneasy about another matter—how was I to bring the machine down?

I sweated nervously about this until the pilot crumpled up his dinner wrapping, and said:

"Now, if you don't mind, I'll bring this bus on down. I know this airport like the back of my hand, because I live here. You have never been here before. So I'll bring you safely to port."

When we were on the ground, I thanked the co-pilot for his flying lessons. I appreciated his services no end.

The forgiveness of sins is rather like someone taking a blackboard. with all his sins written thereon, then seeing a wet sponge wipe it clear.

But the problem of living a righteous life remains. A converted sinner soon finds that he does not possess in himself the power to live a Christian life.

Jesus Christ, departing from His disciples, said: "I will pray the Father, and he will give you another Counselor, to be with you for ever."

This Helper, designated by this Greek word "para-cletos," is the Ambassador of God and the Representative of Christ, in the heart of every believer. "Para-cletos" means "one who stands alongside to help," and that, in the language of the mid-Twentieth Century, could be translated "co-pilot," for truly the functions of a co-pilot are similar. A co-pilot stands alongside to help: the pilot is still in control. A co-pilot who is a pilot-instructor will give directions and guidance: he will correct and advise; and, in the case of the New Hampshire pilot, he will bring the traveler safely to his destination in the unknown.

Who is this Co-Pilot on the heaven-bound way? Christ called Him "the Spirit of Truth." From other Scriptures, we learn that He has intellect, will, and emotion—He can think for Himself, act for Himself and feel in Himself—so He is a real "person," not a thing. (Hypostasis makes a better word, for physical personality is not meant.)

We find that He is omnipotent, omniscient, and omnipresent—all powerful, all knowing, everywhere present—but these are attributes of Deity, for neither angels nor demons, men nor animals are omnipotent, omniscient or omnipresent. The Holy Spirit is therefore God.

And His ministry is to convince the world of sin, guide believers into all truth, and glorify Jesus Christ. Only the Divine Helper can do this.

How can the Holy Spirit be a "person" and yet be God? This is a mystery, hard to explain. Take another mystery: a man is three-fold: body, soul and spirit—all three. How can he be three?

An Indian student approached me in Calcutta during the great Harringay Crusade in London.

"Sahib," he said, "do you know Beelee Gram?"

"Beelee Gram," I repeated. "I don't think so."

"Someone told me that you were a close friend of Beelee Gram!" he protested.

"Not me," said I. Then I understood. "Oh, you mean Billy Graham!"

"That's what I said," he added. "Beelee Gram!"

I assured him that I indeed had known Billy Graham for many years, so he asked me what Billy Graham was like.

"Billy Graham," I explained, "is six feet two, blond, open-faced, deep-set eyes . . ."

He interrupted me.

"Please, sahib. I do not want a 'Hollywood' description . . ."

"Well," I said, "Billy Graham is a great soul. I have never known him to say an unkind word about anyone. He has a remarkable spirit. The London newspapermen were lying in wait for him, but he won them over by his humble spirit."

Unwittingly, I had described a popular figure as body, soul, and spirit, one personality: but this is a mystery beyond comprehension.

Likewise, we add up all that the Scriptures say about the Father: we find that He is the eternal Father; we add up all that the Scriptures say about the Son: we find that He is the eternal Son; we add up all that the Scriptures say about the Spirit: we find that He is the eternal Spirit—one God.

A professor asked our class in Chicago:

"Now, men, do you understand the Trinity?"

There was complete silence. Then a country lad raised his hand to encourage the professor.

"I'm beginning to understand it, sir."

The professor threw up his hands.

"Men, I contend that no one can understand the Trinity. Gentlemen, if you could comprehend the nature of the Godhead, God would not be any greater than the scope of your little mind!"

"Then how can anyone know anything about God?" asked the student.

"We can only know," said the professor, "just as much as God has chosen to reveal to us, and we know that He has revealed Himself to us as Father, Son, and Holy Spirit!"

What illustration is there of the essential oneness —and the essential threeness of the Godhead? St. Patrick plucked a leaf of shamrock to show to the pagan Irish, but there are four-leaved shamrocks. A friend of mine suggested a three-fold cord—but such a rope is only three cords temporarily joined together, capable of separation.

A college president in Boston suggested an illustration—In Space, there is length, breadth, and depth, with no other measurement which cannot be stated in one or other of those dimensions. There is also Time, which is future, present and past, in an essential threeness-in-oneness. In matter there is found also energy, motion and phenomena, three-in-one, one-in-three.

The Universe is comprised of Space, Time, and Matter, the three-in-one. And each of these is presented, not as a way of acting, but as a mode of being. This is the only analogy of the Triune God which meets the essential points of comparison, threeness, oneness, being.

IX

THE REGENERATION OF HEART

To some, being a christian is a matter of birth. They feel that if they are born into a Christian home, and are brought up in a Christian family, that makes them Christians.

I remember riding in a taxi with a Filipino driver. My companion asked the cheerful fellow if he were a Christian. He said: "Sure. My name is Pedro." He had been given the name of a saint and everything was in order.

Others think that being a Christian is a matter of believing, of assent to proper doctrine.

I flew into Chicago one day, and went to see an old professor. He was surprised.

"Where did you come from?" he asked.

"California!" I replied.

"When did you leave there?" he asked.

"This morning," I replied.

"Isn't aviation wonderful?" he commented.

I asked him why he did not make use of it.

"No," he explained. "When it comes to transportation, I am old-fashioned. I go by train!"

"Don't you believe that planes are safe enough?"

"It isn't that," he said. "I know that air insurance isn't much more expensive than rail insurance."

"Are you afraid that the pilot might take you somewhere else?" I inquired, facetiously.

"No, it isn't that either," he smiled.

"Look," I said. "It takes two and a half days to travel from Chicago to Los Angeles by train, and only a half day by plane. On a round trip, you'd save two days going and two days coming, and that's a lot to a busy traveler like you!"

"I know, I know," he said. "I believe in aviation, but not enough to want to fly. I think I'll continue to travel by train as nature intended."

His faith in aviation went no further than mental assent, whereas regular travelers blithely credit the air lines' claims and commit themselves.

Some hold that being a Christian is a matter of philosophy. They think that they simply need to decide that the Christian philosophy is better than any other. This is not enough. For example, I know a Norwegian living in the United States. He believes in democracy, in the rights of man, in religious liberty, in freedom to maintain life, liberty and the pursuit of happiness. But he still cannot vote in a state or national election, for the simple reason that he has not become a citizen. Likewise, holding a Christian philosophy is not enough to make a man a Christian.

Some think that being a Christian is a matter of ethics. They hold the Christian ethic best.

Mahatma Gandhi accepted the ten commandments, and practiced the Sermon on the Mount, but the very year that he was assassinated he wrote a letter to Dr. Stanley Jones and stated that he could not become a Christian.

Some people say that being a Christian is a matter of making profession. They think that the question is settled by formally joining a church.

Christ Himself said:

" 'It is not everyone who keeps saying to me, "Lord,

Lord" who will enter the kingdom of Heaven, but the man who actually does my Heavenly Father's will.' " [1]

What is a true Christian?

The Apostle Paul penned a scriptural definition:

"For if a man is in Christ he becomes a new person altogether—the past is finished and gone, everything has become fresh and new." [2]

The Christian is a person who has enjoyed a transforming experience of the grace of God, as a result of which his life is changed.

What about his old life?

The very first word of the Good News of Jesus Christ is the word "Repent." When John the Baptist began to preach, his message was "Repent, for the kingdom of heaven is at hand." And when Jesus Christ began to preach, He preached the same word first: "Repent, for the kingdom of heaven is at hand." This is the first word of the gospel.

The English word "repentance" is very much misunderstood. The original Greek word, which is "metanoia," is a much stronger concept than is conveyed in its Latin or English translations. Repentance does not mean "feeling sorry." Rather it means to "change one's thinking, change one's ways, change one's feelings."

I heard of a thief who made a speciality of snatching women's handbags. He would look out for a lady window-shopping along the street. He would start running to gain momentum, give the preoccupied woman a hard push, enough to make her lose her balance but not enough to knock her down. Then he would snatch her handbag from her slackened grasp. The thief respected the memory of his mother, and he did not really enjoy pushing old ladies. So, as he sped

[1] J. B. Phillips, *op. cit.*, Matt. vii, 21.   [2] *Ibid*, II Cor. v, 17.

away, he made a ready practice of shouting "Sorry!" And he did feel sorry—but he did not change his ways.

The Apostle Peter began his work at Pentecost by preaching, "Repent . . . and be converted, that your sins may be blotted out, when the times of refreshing shall come from the presence of the Lord."

The Apostle Paul began his ministry by declaring first at Damascus, then at Jerusalem and throughout the whole country of Judea, and also to the Gentiles, "that they should repent and turn to God and perform deeds worthy of their repentance." This was more than feeling sorry.

The first word of the Good News is therefore "Repent!"—"Change your thinking, change your ways." And this repentance is expressed in true conversion, which means simply turning from sin to God. Salvation, said Christ, was unobtainable "except ye be converted!" (K.J.V.)

The basic ingredient of conversion is faith. It must be true faith, for "What does it profit . . . if a man says he has faith but has not works? Can his faith save him?"

The Christian is not saved by faith and works: rather he is saved by the kind of faith that works. He must put his trust in the Lord Jesus Christ, for ". . . to all who received him, who believed in his name, he gave power to become children of God."

The dictionary gives several definitions of this word "believe"—"to have faith"—"to give mental assent"—"to think"—"to judge"—"to hold as true"—"to suppose"—"to hold as one's opinion."

The scriptural use of the verb "to believe" is much more definite and explicit. "Believing" to the Apostles meant "unqualified acceptance of, and exclusive dependence upon" Jesus Christ.

The name Jesus denoted "Savior." The angel of the Lord announced His birth with the words: "You shall call his name Jesus, for he will save his people from their sins."

To "believe on his name" therefore is to make unqualified acceptance of and exclusive dependence upon the Lord Jesus Christ. This means to trust Him fully, to commit oneself to Him wholly—and a Christian is one who belongs to Christ.

To "receive Him" as Savior is as simple an act as one may see at a wedding ceremony any day—the bride by simple declaration receives the man of her choice to be her husband. She not only receives him by word, but commits her life into his care as husband. Receiving Christ as Savior puts the believer in His care as One Who will save him from his sins.

The Holy Spirit of God then begins to indwell the heart and life of the believer, justifying him (acquitting him of guilt, restoring him to right) and sanctifying him (setting him apart for God and from evil) and preparing him for the day of full salvation, body, soul and spirit.

The real evidence of the New Birth is the New Life. If any man is truly a Christian, "he is a new creation; for the old has passed away, . . . the new has come."

What then is required of a seeking sinner? He is commanded by God to change his attitude and ways, to turn to God from sin, to put his whole trust in the Lord Jesus Christ for pardon and to receive transforming power in his heart from the Holy Spirit.

The Scripture promises that his sins will be forgiven, that he will be set right before God, and that His Savior and Lord will begin this work of grace in his heart which He guarantees to perform to the end.

X

THE DECISION OF THE WILL

THERE ARE TWO THINGS which are important in all formal decisions of life—the intention and the declaration.

When an immigrant seeks naturalization, he must first of all notify the appropriate person of his intention privately, after which he must affirm his oath of allegiance before witnesses publicly.

In seeking to marry, a young man must first notify the appropriate person of his intention, privately (and receive a license), after which, when residence requirements are fulfilled, he must declare his vows before witnesses publicly in a church or appropriate office.

In academic life, an applicant must first notify the registrar of the university of his intention, and then (when approved) matriculate publicly.

In military life, a candidate for a commission must notify the military authorities privately of his intention, and follow it up by taking the oath before witnesses publicly.

These things are common knowledge among civilized peoples, but on one occasion I made the mistake of speaking about them to the hill tribes of Kerala, a former slave-people. They knew little about "decision," for they never had occasion to appear before notaries, nor did they make decisions to marry—this was done for them—nor did any ever proceed beyond the first few grades of school, nor were they eligible for the army in India: they were illiterate.

Decisions are made by people daily, weekly, monthly, annually. A family makes a decision to go away for a vacation each summer, but the effects of the decision last for only a week or two. A young man decides to enroll in a course of liberal arts, but that affects his life for only three or four years. In wartime, a fellow applies for a commission, but his decision is effective for the duration of the war and six months beyond. Even when a man is married, the decision made by him is "for as long as you both shall live." But when a person decides to become a Christian, that decision (if Divinely confirmed) is for this life and the life to come. It is indeed life's most important decision.

I began my career as a journalist in the late 1920's as a sports reporter for Ireland's *Saturday Night,* a weekly sports newspaper of the *Belfast Telegraph.* The sports editor had a simple maxim—"get the facts!" Who, why, how, what, where and when?—those were the questions. The subeditor was ready to rewrite copy into more acceptable phrases, but he was helpless without the facts to help his understanding.

It is our purpose, therefore, to suggest five simple questions:

Who must make the decision?
Why must the decision be made?
How must the decision be made?
What must the decision involve?
Where and when must the decisions be made?

The answers to these five questions are found in the writings of the Apostle Paul, the Epistle to the Romans, chapter x, verses 8-13:[1]

"For the secret is very near you, in *your own heart,* in *your own mouth.*" It is the secret of faith,

[1] J. B. Phillips, *op. cit.*

which is the burden of our preaching, and it says, in effect, "If you openly admit by *your own mouth* that Jesus Christ is the Lord, and if you believe in *your own heart* that God raised him from the dead, you will be saved." For it is believing *in the heart* that makes a man righteous before God, and it is stating his belief by *his own mouth* that confirms his salvation. And the scripture says: "Whosoever believes in him shall not be disappointed." And that "whosoever" means anyone, without distinction between Jew or Greek. For all have the same Lord, whose boundless resources are available to all who turn to him in faith. For: "Whosoever shall call upon the name of the Lord shall be saved."

Who? Why? How? What? Where and When? Who must make the decision?

The Apostle rightly insists that "whosoever" means "anyone." There is no distinction between Jew and Greek. The Apostle was not referring to citizenship for in those days both Jew and Greek were subjects of the Roman emperor. He was referring to religious tradition, for in those days the Jew was a God-fearing man, the Greek was a godless[2] man; the Jew was a churchgoing man, the Greek was a pleasure-seeking man; the Jew was a religious man, the Greek less religious.

Today, we have the same classes of people: those who are naturally religious, and those who could not care less; those who attend the Lord's house on the Lord's day, and those who seek pleasure at every opportunity; those who fear God, and those who live as if God did not exist.

Everyone's necessity to decide upsets churchgoing men more than the irreligious. A fellow told me, indig-

[2] So far as Jehovah was concerned.

nantly: "Why don't you talk to some old drunk on skid row? I go to church already!"

Some time ago, a pollster polled the American public on their religious practice: a whopping 85% claimed that they lived their lives according to the Good Book, the Ten Commandments and the Sermon on the Mount! However, 80% declared that 90% of their neighbors did not live rightly, and that statistic almost cancelled the other. Church-going is popular in America.

What is true of the Christian community in the United States is also true of the whole Christian community in India, although a tiny minority.

An Indian student once approached me, saying:
"Sahib, I enjoyed your sermon."
"Thank you," I smiled. "Are you a Christian?"
"Oh, yes," he replied. "I am a Christian."
"How long have you been a Christian?" I asked.
"All my life!" he replied.
"But," I persisted, "surely you have had some personal experience—you have been converted, or confirmed your faith in some way?"
"Sahib," he explained. "You do not understand. It was not I that was converted. It was my great-great-great-great-grandfather. He was converted and brought the whole family into the Christian faith. So, not only am I a Christian, but I come from a whole line of Christians!"
"Splendid!" said I. "Supposing you saw a young couple at breakfast in the Taj Mahal Hotel. You ask the young man, tactfully 'How long have you been married?' 'Married?' he says. 'We are not married. But our parents were married. Our grandparents were married. Our great-grandparents were married, and we both come from a long line of married people!' Is that enough?"

My Indian friend grinned and saw the point. It is a good thing to have forebears who give us a hearty respect for marriage, but each must make his own decision in the matter.

Why must the decision be made?

The Apostle declares, "It is believing *in the heart* that makes a man righteous before God, and it is stating his belief by *his own mouth* that confirms his salvation."[3]

The declaration makes clear that a man is not righteous and that he needs salvation. That there is something wrong with human nature is obvious. That it needs setting right (justifying) is not always so obvious to people.

Talking about setting things right, I recall that I was once showing a motion picture of missionary interest in some church hall in Los Angeles. The projector was placed on a high table which was placed in turn on a lower table, from which I operated the projector, giving a running commentary as the color film ran through.

I happened to lose my balance and fell backwards, descending upon a chair, the point of which made a very painful impression upon the end of my spine. It was ten minutes before I recovered enough breath to continue narrating.

Two months later, I was the house guest of a doctor in the city of Seattle in Washington.

"I don't know why it is," I told him, "that I am suffering from such persistent headaches. It is not my eyes, and it is not my digestion."

The doctor gave me a thorough examination, and agreed that heart, lungs, digestion, blood pressure and other tests were in order. Then he happened to suggest:

[3] J. B. Phillips, *op. cit.*, Romans x, 10.

"Let me look at your spine!"

He played his fingers up and down my spine, like a pianist playing Beethoven's Minuet in G. Then he said:

"Orr, you have four vertebræ out of line! Were you in an automobile crash?"

I told him no.

"Well, then, did you fall downstairs?"

Again I denied it.

"You must have had some kind of accident!"

I assured him that I had not. Then I recalled the projection accident in Los Angeles.

"Down in Los Angeles," I began, "I sat on a chair . . ."

"Oh, I wouldn't let that bother you," he said. "Lots of people have been known to sit on chairs."

"But not the way I did!" I replied, adding the details of the accident. He agreed immediately that this could have been the cause of damage to the spine, that the displaced vertebræ were no doubt impinging upon the nerve endings. He gave me a treatment, and within twenty-four hours the headaches went away.

"Confessing with his mouth" (stating his belief by his own mouth) according to the Apostle Paul, confirms a man's salvation. A man needs to be saved. This is a term disliked by many people. They do not realize that they are lost, hence they feel no need to be saved.

When a sister-in-law of mine was making her arrangements to accompany her husband up into Central Africa, the immigration doctor sent for her husband, and told him that his wife's X-ray had indicated no tuberculosis, but that something else was showing, and should be checked as soon as they arrived at their destination.

The checkup at the hospital in the interior showed a

rapidly spreading cancer. The doctor gave his opinion that the dying woman must have had cancer for a dozen years without knowing it. A Melbourne specialist told me that he wished that cancer were more painful, and, when I looked shocked, added that he meant that he wished that it were more painful in the early stages when it might be remedied.

People are very reluctant to admit that they suffer from the cancer of sin. They like to think that their troubles are benign, not malignant. It is nevertheless incontrovertible that Scripture teaches that Sin is deadly, and that there is no cure for it, apart from the repentance and the conversion of the sinner. A sinner needs to be saved from his sins. He needs the forgiveness—offered in Christ—of his sins.

Why must decision be made? One's life is in danger. Just as a surgeon will not operate without the permission of the patient, who must then decide, so God invites sinners to decide (repent).

How must decision be made?

We all need "to believe in our hearts and to confess with our mouths." The Apostle Paul is so emphatic about this that he repeats the idea four times, mentioning "believing in the heart" and "confessing with the mouth" in verses 8, 9, 10, 12, and verse 11 when combined with verse 13.

We have already pointed out that most formal decisions involve a proper intention made known privately, and a proper declaration made known publicly. So it is with decision for Christ.

Believing in the heart, and confessing with the mouth! It must be both. Some people will do one and not the other. There are those who will make their public profession of faith, such as is expected in joining a church, yet they know that they do not really believe in their hearts that they are saved. Others believe the facts of the Gospel in their hearts, but they will not confess with their mouths. It must be both.

At the end of World War II, I attended a wedding of a friend of mine. There was something about the attitude of the bride which caused me uneasiness, and I was not at all surprised when the bridegroom came to me a month later and said that he was in trouble.

It was so serious, he said, that his bride had not spoken to him on their way to the place of the honeymoon. I asked him if they were living together as husband and wife. He answered no! He asked me if I thought that he should arrange to divorce her. He saw no future happiness.

In the meantime, I had discovered that the girl had been on bad terms with her own mother. The rebel had told her mother that she was going to walk out and get an apartment of her own.

"Let's see you get a place of your own," said the mother. "You know, my girl, that so many houses were destroyed in the blitz that only an ex-serviceman newly-wed can get a vacancy."

The young lady went through a form of marriage with my friend, got herself an apartment thereby, and then refused to keep her marriage vows. I told my friend that he should not divorce her, but that under the circumstances any judge would annul a marriage contracted without honest intention.

The opposite is also true. In Ireland, I knew a young lady who was engaged to be married. Her fiance was honorable in his intentions, but he was very shy of a wedding ceremony. Every time she said: "Joe, why don't we get married next month?" he became so scared, he fled, and did not return for a fortnight. When I knew them, they had been engaged to be married for seventeen years. He had honest intentions, but he was unwilling to make the proper declaration publicly.

To make the decision for Christ, there must be the private intention in the heart, and there must be the public declaration of the mouth.

What must the decision involve?

The Apostle Paul declares: "If you confess with your lips that Jesus is Lord and believe in your heart that God raised Him from the dead, you will be saved."

The decision does not concern a religion; it involves a person. It does not say that to be a Christian one must accept the Ten Commandments and the Sermon on the Mount! It does not say that one must accept the Apostles' Creed! It declares that one must accept a person —as Lord, and as alive today.

At a meeting in the University of Chicago, a young lady raised her hand to say:

"I don't understand this. If a man believes in Communism, he is a Communist; if he believes in Socialism, he is a Socialist: well, I believe in Christianity—am I not a Christian?"

"Not necessarily so," I replied.

I noticed that she was wearing an engagement ring, so I asked:

"Could I ask you a personal question?"

"Certainly," she replied.

"Do you believe in marriage?"

"Of course I believe in marriage!" she replied. "I'm engaged to be married."

"Can you give me any good reasons for it?"

"Marriage," she said, "gives a woman a home and a family, a career and social prestige . . ."

Facetiously, I asked the young ladies in the company

present how many of them believed in marriage, and they all gigglingly raised their hands—except one determined spinster.

"That's very interesting," said I. "You all say that you believe in marriage as an institution or a philosophy. It so happens that I am a chaplain of the United States Air Force. I am recognized by state government to perform marriages. This young lady says if one believes in Communism, he is a Communist; if one believes in Christianity, he is a Christian; now you all tell me you believe in marriage: allow me to pronounce you married."

That was greeted with hoots of derision.

"What's wrong with that?" I asked.

"Mr. Orr," protested one girl, patiently, "you know that marriage is not a philosophy; marriage is a personal relationship!"

"Exactly," I returned. "And Christianity is not a mere philosophy; to be a Christian is a personal relationship with Jesus Christ, a living Person."

The Scripture declares that to be saved, one must confess with his mouth that Jesus Christ is Lord. Many people will confess that Jesus Christ is a great man; most will confess that He is a great teacher; some will say that He is a great martyr: but the Scripture says that, to be saved, one must confess that He is the Lord.

The Scripture declares that to be saved, one must believe in his heart that God raised Christ from the dead. This means that Jesus Christ is alive now, therefore able to help all who call.

One of our planes was shot down near Borneo. Our Air-Sea Rescue squadron searched the ocean for three fruitless weeks for the pilot. They found an oilslick and the wreckage of the plane on the water, but no sign of a rubber dinghy or the pilot. Either he had been eaten by sharks or had been killed by the Japanese. He was first posted as "missing," then, after due interval, as "dead."

A year later, the Australian infantry invaded Borneo. Our fighter group gave them cover from the Philippine island of Palawan. I heard a rumor that this pilot had been discovered among Dyak tribesmen—alive though emaciated.

He was repatriated to San Francisco. His wife was notified by War Department telegram of her husband's recovery. But, as his family name of Jones was so very common, she could not at first credit the good news. Then she received a personal telephone call from her husband in San Francisco.

A group pilot returning on rotation to the same city called to see his comrade's wife. He assured her that he had seen the pilot in a hospital in San Francisco, that he was soon to be on his way to her, and he offered to show her their military orders to prove that it was her husband who had been returned from the dead. The rejoicing girl protested happily that she needed no proof. She had heard her husband's voice.

Where and when must the decision be made?

" 'The secret,' declares the Apostle, 'is very near you, in *your own heart,* in *your own mouth!*' It is the secret of faith . . ."[4]

The word "very near you" ("nigh thee" in the King James Version) means literally "within your reach," "within your grasp."

During the Battle of Manila, I was trying to sleep in a miserable tent which contained twenty-five army cots. There were twenty-three other officers in that tent, and there is always one frog to start the croaking

[4] J. B. Phillips, *op. cit.,* Romans x, 8.

—too soon all twenty-three men were snoring, some bass, some baritone, some tenor.

I tried hard to sleep, but I could not succeed. I tried to count numbers, but sleep eluded me. I quoted verses of poetry, but still I was wide awake. I recited verses of Scripture, without avail. The barrage of snoring was more bother than the barrages of artillery in the distance, pounding the old city section of Manila into rubble.

At two in the morning, I heard a step on the gravel path. It was a pilot, looking for a bed. He was tired and he was hungry.

As he came under the tent, he heard the barrage of snoring, and let out a string of words of an improper sort. Then he asked rhetorically:

"Where is that light?"

He did not expect an answer, for, when my voice struck his ears in the darkness, he jumped.

'If you stand right where you are," I said, "and reach out your right hand, you'll find a cord . . ."

"Just tell me where it is, man," he barked.

And he added a stream of profanity.

"Don't swear at me," said I. "I'm trying to tell you and you won't even listen to me."

He could have sworn all night and it would not have helped him. He could have asked me how the tent was wired electrically, and I could not have told him. He could have asked me to explain how a current of electricity, passed through a filament in a vacuum, could radiate light; and I could not have told him. All he needed to do was to take my word for it, pull the suspended cord, watch the light come on, and find that there was enough illumination to show him all he needed to see. The answer to his problem was within reach.

The secret of believing is within one's reach. Put it off till one is married: it is still the same decision—to believe in the heart and confess with the mouth. Put it off till one's family is grown: it is still the same decision—to believe in the heart and confess with the mouth. Put it off till one retires: it is still the same decision—to believe in the heart and confess with the mouth. Put it off till one's deathbed: it is still the same decision—to believe in the heart and confess with the mouth. The decision for Christ is as close just now as it ever will be—it is very near you.

On our honeymoon in the foothills of the great Drakensberg range in Africa, I asked my bride (to satisfy my curiosity) when she actually made up her mind to marry me, for I had proposed so often. She told me: It was not the same day that she had let me know—it was the day before. Why? She had wanted to be very sure.

So she made her decision in the secret of her heart. That was the first step. Then she told me, the person most concerned, the second step. She with me told her mother, her best friend, the third step. That evening, at supper, she told of our engagement to her family . . . And the final step was when she took the vows of marriage in a public ceremony, before witnesses. Then we lived happily ever afterwards.

Likewise, the first step of a decision for Christ—to repent of sin and turn to God and believe the Good News of salvation—must be realized in the secret of the heart. Too often zealous Christians expect the seeker to make a public declaration before he has made a secret decision. The next step for the majority of people is to tell Christ, the Person most concerned, for "every one who calls upon the name of the Lord will be saved."

The usual step for most people is to tell a good friend. Then one confesses Christ to a circle of friends. Finally, the confession of faith in Christ can be made publicly, before all men. And if we confess Him before men, He will confess us before God.